O'REILLY®
Strata
Making Data Work

T0221562

Learn how ~~to turn~~ data into decisions.

From startups to the Fortune 500, smart companies are betting on data-driven insight, seizing the opportunities that are emerging from the convergence of four powerful trends:

- New methods of collecting, managing, and analyzing data

- Cloud computing that offers inexpensive storage and flexible, on-demand computing power for massive data sets

- Visualization techniques that turn complex data into images that tell a compelling story

- Tools that make the power of data available to anyone

Get control over big data and turn it into insight with O'Reilly's Strata offerings. Find the inspiration and information to create new products or revive existing ones, understand customer behavior, and get the data edge.

O'REILLY®

Visit oreilly.com/data to learn more.

Parallel R

Q. Ethan McCallum and Stephen Weston

O'REILLY®

Beijing · Cambridge · Farnham · Köln · Sebastopol · Tokyo

Parallel R

by Q. Ethan McCallum and Stephen Weston

Published by O'Reilly Media, Inc., 1005 Gravenstein Highway North, Sebastopol, CA 95472.

O'Reilly books may be purchased for educational, business, or sales promotional use. Online editions are also available for most titles (*http://my.safaribooksonline.com*). For more information, contact our corporate/institutional sales department: (800) 998-9938 or *corporate@oreilly.com*.

Editors: Mike Loukides and Meghan Blanchette
Production Editor: Kristen Borg
Proofreader: O'Reilly Production Services

Cover Designer: Karen Montgomery
Interior Designer: David Futato
Illustrator: Robert Romano

Revision History for the First Edition:
   2011-10-21   First release
See *http://oreilly.com/catalog/errata.csp?isbn=9781449309923* for release details.

ISBN: 978-1-449-30992-3

[LSI]

1319202075

Table of Contents

Preface

Conventions Used in This Book

The following typographical conventions are used in this book:

Italic

Indicates new terms, URLs, email addresses, filenames, and file extensions.

`Constant width`

Used for program listings, as well as within paragraphs to refer to program elements such as variable or function names, databases, data types, environment variables, statements, and keywords.

`Constant width bold`

Shows commands or other text that should be typed literally by the user.

`Constant width italic`

Shows text that should be replaced with user-supplied values or by values determined by context.

This icon signifies a tip, suggestion, or general note.

This icon indicates a warning or caution.

Using Code Examples

This book is here to help you get your job done. In general, you may use the code in this book in your programs and documentation. You do not need to contact us for permission unless you're reproducing a significant portion of the code. For example, writing a program that uses several chunks of code from this book does not require permission. Selling or distributing a CD-ROM of examples from O'Reilly books does require permission. Answering a question by citing this book and quoting example code does not require permission. Incorporating a significant amount of example code from this book into your product's documentation does require permission.

We appreciate, but do not require, attribution. An attribution usually includes the title, author, publisher, and ISBN. For example: "*Parallel R* by Q. Ethan McCallum and Stephen Weston (O'Reilly). Copyright 2012 Q. Ethan McCallum and Stephen Weston, 978-1-449-30992-3."

If you feel your use of code examples falls outside fair use or the permission given above, feel free to contact us at *permissions@oreilly.com*.

Safari® Books Online

Safari Books Online is an on-demand digital library that lets you easily search over 7,500 technology and creative reference books and videos to find the answers you need quickly.

With a subscription, you can read any page and watch any video from our library online. Read books on your cell phone and mobile devices. Access new titles before they are available for print, and get exclusive access to manuscripts in development and post feedback for the authors. Copy and paste code samples, organize your favorites, download chapters, bookmark key sections, create notes, print out pages, and benefit from tons of other time-saving features.

O'Reilly Media has uploaded this book to the Safari Books Online service. To have full digital access to this book and others on similar topics from O'Reilly and other publishers, sign up for free at *http://my.safaribooksonline.com*.

How to Contact Us

Please address comments and questions concerning this book to the publisher:

O'Reilly Media, Inc.
1005 Gravenstein Highway North
Sebastopol, CA 95472
800-998-9938 (in the United States or Canada)
707-829-0515 (international or local)
707-829-0104 (fax)

We have a web page for this book, where we list errata, examples, and any additional information. You can access this page at:

http://oreilly.com/catalog/0636920021421

To comment or ask technical questions about this book, send email to:

bookquestions@oreilly.com

For more information about our books, courses, conferences, and news, see our website at *http://www.oreilly.com*.

Find us on Facebook: *http://facebook.com/oreilly*

Follow us on Twitter: *http://twitter.com/oreillymedia*

Watch us on YouTube: *http://www.youtube.com/oreillymedia*

Acknowledgments

There are only two names on the cover, but a host of people made this book possible.

We would like to thank the entire O'Reilly team for their efforts. They provided such a smooth process that we were able to focus on just the writing. A special thanks goes to our editors, Mike Loukides and Meghan Blanchette, for their guidance and support.

We would also like to thank our review team. The following people generously dedicated their time and energy to read this book in its early state, and their feedback helped shape the text into the finished product you're reading now:

> Robert Bjornson
> Nicholas Carriero
> Jonathan Seidman
> Paul Teetor
> Ramesh Venkataramaiah
> Jed Wing

Any errors you find in this book belong to us, the authors.

Most of all we thank you, the reader, for your interest in this book. We set out to create the guidebook we wish we'd had when we first tried to give R that parallel, distributed boost. R work is research work, best done with minimal distractions. We hope these chapters help you get up to speed quickly, so you can get R to do what you need with minimal detour from the task at hand.

Q. Ethan McCallum

"You like math? Oh, you need to talk to Mike. Let me introduce you." I didn't realize it at the time, but those words were the start of this project. Really. A chance encounter with Mike Loukides led to emails and phone calls and, before I knew it, we'd laid the groundwork for a new book. So first and foremost, a hearty thanks to Betsy and Laurel, who made my connection to Mike.

Conversations with Mike led me to my co-author, Steve Weston. I'm pleased and flattered that he agreed to join me on this adventure.

Thanks as well to the gang at Cafe les Deux Chats, for providing a quiet place to work.

Stephen Weston

This was my first book project, so I'd like to thank my co-author and editors for putting up with my freshman confusion and mistakes. They were very gracious throughout the project.

I'm very grateful to Nick, Rob, and Jed for taking the time to read my chapters and help me not to make a fool of myself. I also want to thank my wife Diana and daughter Erica for proofreading material that wasn't on their preferred reading lists.

Finally, I'd like to thank all the authors of the packages that we discuss in this book. I had a lot of fun reading the source for all three of the packages that I wrote about. In particular, I've always loved the snow source code, which I studied when first learning to program in R.

## CHAPTER 1

Getting Started

This chapter sets the pace for the rest of the book. If you're in a hurry, feel free to skip to the chapter you need. (The section "In a Hurry?" on page 4 has a quick-ref look at the various strategies and where they fit. That should help you pick a starting point.) Just make sure you come back here to understand our choice of vocabulary, how we chose what to cover, and so on.

Why R?

It's tough to argue with R. Who could dislike a high-quality, cross-platform, open-source statistical software product? It has an interactive console for exploratory work. It can run as a scripting language to repeat a process you've captured. It has a lot of statistical calculations built-in so you don't have to reinvent the wheel. Did we mention that R is *free*?

When the base toolset isn't enough, R users have access to a rich ecosystem of add-on packages and a gaggle of GUIs to make their lives even easier. No wonder R has become a favorite in the age of Big Data.

Since R is perfect, then, we can end this book. Right?

Not quite. It's precisely the Big Data age that has exposed R's blemishes.

Why Not R?

These imperfections stem not from defects in the software itself, but from the passage of time: quite simply, R was not built in anticipation of the Big Data revolution.

R was born in 1995. Disk space was expensive, RAM even more so, and this thing called The Internet was just getting its legs. Notions of "large-scale data analysis" and "high-performance computing" were reasonably rare. Outside of Wall Street firms and university research labs, there just wasn't that much data to crunch.

Fast-forward to the present day and hardware costs just a fraction of what it used to. Computing power is available online for pennies. Everyone is suddenly interested in collecting and analyzing data, and the necessary resources are well within reach.

This surge in data analysis has brought two of R's limitations to the forefront: it's *single-threaded* and *memory-bound*. Allow us to explain:

It's single-threaded
> The R language has no explicit constructs for parallelism, such as threads or mutexes. An out-of-the-box R install cannot take advantage of multiple CPUs.

It's memory-bound
> R requires that your entire dataset* fit in memory (RAM).† Four gigabytes of RAM will not hold eight gigabytes of data, no matter how much you smile when you ask.

While these are certainly inconvenient, they're hardly insurmountable.

The Solution: Parallel Execution

People have created a series of workarounds over the years. Doing a lot of matrix math? You can build R against a multithreaded basic linear algebra subprogram (BLAS). Churning through large datasets? Use a relational database or another manual method to retrieve your data in smaller, more manageable pieces. And so on, and so forth.

Some big winners involve *parallelism*. Spreading work across multiple CPUs overcomes R's single-threaded nature. Offloading work to multiple machines reaps the multi-process benefit and also addresses R's memory barrier. In this book we'll cover a few strategies to give R that parallel boost, specifically those which take advantage of modern multicore hardware and cheap distributed computing.

A Road Map for This Book

Now that we've set the tone for why we're here, let's take a look at what we plan to accomplish in the coming pages (or screens if you're reading this electronically).

---

* We emphasize "dataset" here, not necessarily "algorithms."

† It's a big problem. Because R will often make multiple copies of the same data structure for no apparent reason, you often need three times as much memory as the size of your dataset. And if you don't have enough memory, you die a slow death as your poor machine swaps and thrashes. Some people turn off virtual memory with the `swapoff` command so they can die quickly.

What We'll Cover

Each chapter is a look into one strategy for R parallelism, including:

- What it is
- Where to find it
- How to use it
- Where it works well, and where it doesn't

First up is the `snow` package, followed by a tour of the `multicore` package. We then provide a look at the new `parallel` package that's due to arrive in R 2.14. After that, we'll take a brief side-tour to explain MapReduce and Hadoop. That will serve as a foundation for the remaining chapters: R+Hadoop (Hadoop streaming and the Java API), RHIPE, and `segue`.

Looking Forward...

In Chapter 9, we will briefly mention some tools that were too new for us to cover in-depth.

There will likely be other tools we hadn't heard about (or that didn't exist) at the time of writing.‡ Please let us know about them! You can reach us through this book's website at *http://parallelrbook.com/*.

What We'll Assume You Already Know

This is a book about R, yes, but we'll expect you know the basics of how to get around. If you're new to R or need a refresher course, please flip through Paul Teetor's *R Cookbook* (O'Reilly), Robert Kabacoff's *R In Action* (Manning), or another introductory title. You should take particular note of the `lapply()` function, which plays an important role in this book.

Some of the topics require several machines' worth of infrastructure, in which case you'll need access to a talented sysadmin. You'll also need hardware, which you can buy and maintain yourself, or rent from a hosting provider. Cloud services, notably Amazon Web Services (AWS), § have become a popular choice in this arena. AWS has plenty of documentation, and you can also read *Programming Amazon EC2*, by Jurg van Vliet and Flavia Paganelli (O'Reilly) as a supplement.

(Please note that using a provider still requires a degree of sysadmin knowledge. If you're not up to the task, you'll want to find and bribe your skilled sysadmin friends.)

---

‡ Try as we might, our massive Monte Carlo simulations have brought us no closer to predicting the next R parallelism strategy. Nor any winning lottery numbers, for that matter.

§ *http://aws.amazon.com/*

In a Hurry?

If you're in a hurry, you can skip straight to the chapter you need. The list below is a quick look at the various strategies.

snow

Overview: Good for use on traditional clusters, especially if MPI is available. It supports MPI, PVM, nws, and sockets for communication, and is quite portable, running on Linux, Mac OS X, and Windows.

Solves: Single-threaded, memory-bound.

Pros: Mature, popular package; leverages MPI's speed without its complexity.

Cons: Can be difficult to configure.

multicore

Overview: Good for big-CPU problems when setting up a Hadoop cluster is too much of a hassle. Lets you parallelize your R code without ever leaving the R interpreter.

Solves: Single-threaded.

Pros: Simple and efficient; easy to install; no configuration needed.

Cons: Can only use one machine; doesn't support Windows; no built-in support for parallel random number generation (RNG).

parallel

Overview: A merger of snow and multicore that comes built into R as of R 2.14.0.

Solves: Single-threaded, memory-bound.

Pros: No installation necessary; has great support for parallel random number generation.

Cons: Can only use one machine on Windows; can be difficult to configure on multiple Linux machines.

R+Hadoop

Overview: Run your R code on a Hadoop cluster.

Solves: Single-threaded, memory-bound.

Pros: You get Hadoop's scalability.

Cons: Requires a Hadoop cluster (internal or cloud-based); breaks up a single logical process into multiple scripts and steps (can be a hassle for exploratory work).

RHIPE

Overview: Talk Hadoop without ever leaving the R interpreter.

Solves: Single-threaded, memory-bound.

Pros: Closer to a native R experience than R+Hadoop; use pure R code for your Map-Reduce operations.

Cons: Requires a Hadoop cluster; requires extra setup on the cluster; cannot process standard SequenceFiles (for binary data).

Segue

Overview: Seamlessly send R `apply`-like calculations to a remote Hadoop cluster.

Solves: Single-threaded, memory-bound.

Pros: Abstracts you from Elastic MapReduce management.

Cons: Cannot use with an internal Hadoop cluster (you're tied to Amazon's Elastic MapReduce).

Summary

Welcome to the beginning of your journey into parallel R. Our first stop is a look at the popular snow package.

snow

snow ("Simple Network of Workstations") is probably the most popular parallel programming package available for R. It was written by Luke Tierney, A. J. Rossini, Na Li, and H. Sevcikova, and is actively maintained by Luke Tierney. It is a mature package, first released on the "Comprehensive R Archive Network" (CRAN) in 2003.

Quick Look

Motivation: You want to use a Linux cluster to run an R script faster. For example, you're running a Monte Carlo simulation on your laptop, but you're sick of waiting many hours or days for it to finish.

Solution: Use snow to run your R code on your company or university's Linux cluster.

Good because: snow fits well into a traditional cluster environment, and is able to take advantage of high-speed communication networks, such as InfiniBand, using MPI.

How It Works

snow provides support for easily executing R functions in parallel. Most of the parallel execution functions in snow are variations of the standard `lapply()` function, making snow fairly easy to learn. To implement these parallel operations, snow uses a master/worker architecture, where the master sends tasks to the workers, and the workers execute the tasks and return the results to the master.

One important feature of snow is that it can be used with different transport mechanisms to communicate between the master and workers. This allows it to be portable, but still take advantage of high-performance communication mechanisms if available. snow can be used with socket connections, MPI, PVM, or NetWorkSpaces. The socket transport doesn't require any additional packages, and is the most portable. MPI is supported via the `Rmpi` package, PVM via `rpvm`, and NetWorkSpaces via `nws`. The MPI transport is popular on Linux clusters, and the socket transport is popular on multicore computers, particularly Windows computers.*

snow is primarily intended to run on traditional clusters and is particularly useful if MPI is available. It is well suited to Monte Carlo simulations, bootstrapping, cross validation, ensemble machine learning algorithms, and K-Means clustering.

Good support is available for parallel random number generation, using the rsprng and rlecuyer packages. This is very important when performing simulations, bootstrapping, and machine learning, all of which can depend on random number generation.

snow doesn't provide mechanisms for dealing with large data, such as distributing data files to the workers. The input arguments must fit into memory when calling a snow function, and all of the task results are kept in memory on the master until they are returned to the caller in a list. Of course, snow can be used with high-performance distributed file systems in order to operate on large data files, but it's up to the user to arrange that.

Setting Up

snow is available on CRAN, so it is installed like any other CRAN package. It is pure R code and almost never has installation problems. There are binary packages for both Windows and Mac OS X.

Although there are various ways to install packages from CRAN, I generally use the install.packages() function:

```
install.packages("snow")
```

It may ask you which CRAN mirror to use, and then it will download and install the package.

If you're using an old version of R, you may get a message saying that snow is not available. snow has required R 2.12.1 since version 0.3-5, so you might need to download and install snow 0.3-3 from the CRAN package archives. In your browser, search for "CRAN snow" and it will probably bring you to snow's download page on CRAN. Click on the "snow archive" link, and then you can download snow_0.3-3.tar.gz. Or you can try directly downloading it from:

```
http://cran.r-project.org/src/contrib/Archive/snow/snow_0.3-3.tar.gz
```

Once you've downloaded it, you can install it from the command line with:

```
% R CMD INSTALL snow_0.3-3.tar.gz
```

You may need to use the -l option to specify a different installation directory if you don't have permission to install it in the default directory. For help on this command,

---

* The multicore package is generally preferred on multicore computers, but it isn't supported on Windows. See Chapter 3 for more information on the multicore package.

use the --help option. For more information on installing R packages, see the section "Installing packages" in the "R Installation and Administration" manual, written by the "R Development Core Team", and available from the R Project website.

 As a developer, I always use the most recent version of R. That makes it easier to install packages from CRAN, since packages are only built for the most recent version of R on CRAN. They keep around older binary distributions of packages, but they don't build new packages or new versions of packages for anything but the current version of R. And if a new version of a package depends on a newer version of R, as with snow, you can't even build it for yourself on an older version of R. However, if you're using R for production use, you need to be much more cautious about upgrading to the latest version of R.

To use snow with MPI, you will also need to install the Rmpi package. Unfortunately, installing Rmpi is a frequent cause of problems because it has an external dependency on MPI. For more information, see "Installing Rmpi" on page 29.

Fortunately, the socket transport can be used without installing any additional packages. For that reason, I suggest that you start by using the socket transport if you are new to snow.

Once you've installed snow, you should verify that you can load it:

```
library(snow)
```

If that succeeds, you are ready to start using snow.

Working with It

Creating Clusters with makeCluster

In order to execute any functions in parallel with snow, you must first create a *cluster object*. The cluster object is used to interact with the cluster workers, and is passed as the first argument to many of the snow functions. You can create different types of cluster objects, depending on the transport mechanism that you wish to use.

The basic cluster creation function is makeCluster() which can create any type of cluster. Let's use it to create a cluster of four workers on the local machine using the socket transport:

```
cl <- makeCluster(4, type="SOCK")
```

The first argument is the *cluster specification*, and the second is the *cluster type*. The interpretation of the cluster specification depends on the type, but all cluster types allow you to specify a worker count.

Socket clusters also allow you to specify the worker machines as a character vector. The following will launch four workers on remote machines:

```
spec <- c("n1", "n2", "n3", "n4")
cl <- makeCluster(spec, type="SOCK")
```

The socket transport launches each of these workers via the ssh command[†] unless the name is "localhost", in which case makeCluster() starts the worker itself. For remote execution, you should configure ssh to use password-less login. This can be done using public-key authentication and SSH agents, which is covered in chapter 6 of *SSH, The Secure Shell: The Definitive Guide* (O'Reilly) and many websites.

makeCluster() allows you to specify addition arguments as configuration options. This is discussed further in "snow Configuration" on page 26.

The type argument can be "SOCK", "MPI", "PVM" or "NWS". To create an MPI cluster with four workers, execute:

```
cl <- makeCluster(4, type="MPI")
```

This will start four MPI workers on the local machine unless you make special provisions, as described in the section "Executing snow Programs on a Cluster with Rmpi" on page 30.

You can also use the functions makeSOCKcluster(), makeMPIcluster(), makePVMcluster(), and makeNWScluster() to create specific types of clusters. In fact, makeCluster() is nothing more than a wrapper around these functions.

To shut down any type of cluster, use the stopCluster() function:

```
stopCluster(cl)
```

Some cluster types may be automatically stopped when the R session exits, but it's good practice to always call stopCluster() in snow scripts; otherwise, you risk leaking cluster workers if the cluster type is changed, for example.

 Creating the cluster object can fail for a number of reasons, and is therefore a source of problems. See the section "Troubleshooting snow Programs" on page 33 for help in solving these problems.

Parallel K-Means

We're finally ready to use snow to do some parallel computing, so let's look at a real example: parallel K-Means. K-Means is a clustering algorithm that partitions rows of a dataset into k clusters.[‡] It's an iterative algorithm, since it starts with a guess of the

---

† This can be overridden via the rshcmd option, but the specified command must be command line-compatible with ssh.

‡ These clusters shouldn't be confused with cluster objects and cluster workers.

location for each of the cluster centers, and gradually improves the center locations until it converges on a solution.

R includes a function for performing K-Means clustering in the stats package: the kmeans() function. One way of using the kmeans() function is to specify the number of cluster centers, and kmeans() will pick the starting points for the centers by randomly selecting that number of rows from your dataset. After it iterates to a solution, it computes a value called the *total within-cluster sum of squares*. It then selects another set of rows for the starting points, and repeats this process in an attempt to find a solution with a smallest *total within-cluster sum of squares*.

Let's use kmeans() to generate four clusters of the "Boston" dataset, using 100 random sets of centers:

```
library(MASS)
result <- kmeans(Boston, 4, nstart=100)
```

We're going to take a simple approach to parallelizing kmeans() that can be used for parallelizing many similar functions and doesn't require changing the source code for kmeans(). We simply call the kmeans() function on each of the workers using a smaller value of the nstart argument. Then we combine the results by picking the result with the smallest *total within-cluster sum of squares*.

But before we execute this in parallel, let's try using this technique using the lapply() function to make sure it works. Once that is done, it will be fairly easy to convert to one of the snow parallel execution functions:

```
library(MASS)
results <- lapply(rep(25, 4), function(nstart) kmeans(Boston, 4, nstart=nstart))
i <- sapply(results, function(result) result$tot.withinss)
result <- results[[which.min(i)]]
```

We used a vector of four 25s to specify the nstart argument in order to get equivalent results to using 100 in a single call to kmeans(). Generally, the length of this vector should be equal to the number of workers in your cluster when running in parallel.

Now let's parallelize this algorithm. snow includes a number of functions that we could use, including clusterApply(), clusterApplyLB(), and parLapply(). For this example, we'll use clusterApply(). You call it exactly the same as lapply(), except that it takes a snow cluster object as the first argument. We also need to load MASS on the workers, rather than on the master, since it's the workers that use the "Boston" dataset.

Assuming that snow is loaded and that we have a cluster object named cl, here's the parallel version:

```
ignore <- clusterEvalQ(cl, {library(MASS); NULL})
results <- clusterApply(cl, rep(25, 4), function(nstart) kmeans(Boston, 4,
    nstart=nstart))
i <- sapply(results, function(result) result$tot.withinss)
result <- results[[which.min(i)]]
```

clusterEvalQ() takes two arguments: the cluster object, and an expression that is evaluated on each of the workers. It returns the result from each of the workers in a list, which we don't use here. I use a compound expression to load MASS and return NULL to avoid sending unnecessary data back to the master process. That isn't a serious issue in this case, but it can be, so I often return NULL to be safe.

As you can see, the snow version isn't that much different than the lapply() version. Most of the work was done in converting it to use lapply(). Usually the biggest problem in converting from lapply() to one of the parallel operations is handling the data properly and efficiently. In this case, the dataset was in a package, so all we had to do was load the package on the workers.

 The kmeans() function uses the sample.int() function to choose the starting cluster centers, which depend on the random number generator. In order to get different solutions, the cluster workers need to use different streams of random numbers. Since the workers are randomly seeded when they first start generating random numbers,[§] this example will work, but it is good practice to use a parallel random number generator. See "Random Number Generation" on page 25 for more information.

Initializing Workers

In the last section we used the clusterEvalQ() function to initialize the cluster workers by loading a package on each of them. clusterEvalQ() is very handy, especially for interactive use, but it isn't very general. It's great for executing a simple expression on the cluster workers, but it doesn't allow you to pass any kind of parameters to the expression, for example. Also, although you can use it to execute a function, it won't send that function to the worker first,[||] as clusterApply() does.

My favorite snow function for initializing the cluster workers is clusterCall(). The arguments are pretty simple: it takes a snow cluster object, a worker function, and any number of arguments to pass to the function. It simply calls the function with the specified arguments on each of the cluster workers, and returns the results as a list. It's like clusterApply() without the x argument, so it executes once for each worker, like clusterEvalQ(), rather than once for each element in x.

[§] All R sessions are randomly seeded when they first generate random numbers, unless they were restored from a previous R session that generated random numbers. snow workers never restore previously saved data, so they are always randomly seeded.

[||] How exactly snow sends functions to the workers is a bit complex, raising issues of execution context and environment. See "Functions and Environments" on page 23 for more information.

clusterCall() can do anything that clusterEvalQ() does and more.[#] For example, here's how we could use clusterCall() to load the MASS package on the cluster workers:

```
clusterCall(cl, function() { library(MASS); NULL })
```

This defines a simple function that loads the MASS package and returns NULL.[*] Returning NULL guarantees that we don't accidentally send unnecessary data transfer back to the master.[†]

The following will load several packages specified by a character vector:

```
worker.init <- function(packages) {
  for (p in packages) {
    library(p, character.only=TRUE)
  }
  NULL
}
clusterCall(cl, worker.init, c('MASS', 'boot'))
```

Setting the character.only argument to TRUE makes library() interpret the argument as a character variable. If we didn't do that, library() would attempt to load a package named p repeatedly.

Although it's not as commonly used as clusterCall(), the clusterApply() function is also useful for initializing the cluster workers since it can send different data to the initialization function for each worker. The following creates a global variable on each of the cluster workers that can be used as a unique worker ID:

```
clusterApply(cl, seq(along=cl), function(id) WORKER.ID <<- id)
```

Load Balancing with clusterApplyLB

We introduced the clusterApply() function in the parallel K-Means example. The next parallel execution function that I'll discuss is clusterApplyLB(). It's very similar to clusterApply(), but instead of scheduling tasks in a *round-robin* fashion, it sends new tasks to the cluster workers as they complete their previous task. By round-robin, I mean that clusterApply() distributes the elements of x to the cluster workers one at a time, in the same way that cards are dealt to players in a card game. In a sense, clusterApply() (politely) pushes tasks to the workers, while clusterApplyLB() lets the workers pull tasks as needed. That can be more efficient if some tasks take longer than others, or if some cluster workers are slower.

[#]This is guaranteed since clusterEvalQ() is implemented using clusterCall().

[*] Defining anonymous functions like this is very useful, but can be a source of performance problems due to R's scoping rules and the way it serializes functions. See "Functions and Environments" on page 23 for more information.

[†] The return value from library() isn't big, but if the initialization function was assigning a large matrix to a variable, you could inadvertently send a lot of data back to the master, significantly hurting the performance of your program.

To demonstrate `clusterApplyLB()`, we'll execute `Sys.sleep()` on the workers, giving us complete control over the task lengths. Since our real interest in using `cluster ApplyLB()` is to improve performance, we'll use `snow.time()` to gather timing information about the overall execution.[‡] We will also use `snow.time()`'s plotting capability to visualize the task execution on the workers:

```
set.seed(7777442)
sleeptime <- abs(rnorm(10, 10, 10))
tm <- snow.time(clusterApplyLB(cl, sleeptime, Sys.sleep))
plot(tm)
```

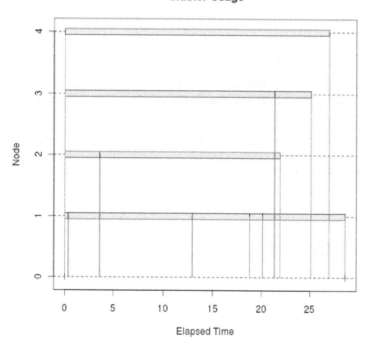

Ideally there would be solid horizontal bars for nodes 1 through 4 in the plot, indicating that the cluster workers were always busy, and therefore running efficiently. `cluster ApplyLB()` did pretty well, although there was some wasted time at the end.

Now let's try the same problem with `clusterApply()`:[§]

```
set.seed(7777442)
sleeptime <- abs(rnorm(10, 10, 10))
tm <- snow.time(clusterApply(cl, sleeptime, Sys.sleep))
plot(tm)
```

[‡] `snow.time()` is available in `snow` as of version 0.3-5.

[§] I'm setting the RNG seed so we get the same value of `sleeptime` as in the previous example.

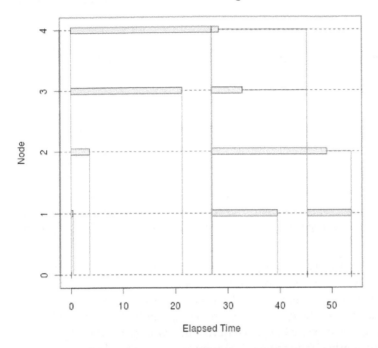

Cluster Usage

As you can see, clusterApply() is much less efficient than clusterApplyLB() in this example: it took 53.7 seconds, versus 28.5 seconds for clusterApplyLB(). The plot shows how much time was wasted due to the round-robin scheduling.

But don't give up on clusterApply(): it has its uses. It worked fine in the parallel K-Means example because we had the same number of tasks as workers. It is also used to implement the very useful parLapply() function, which we will discuss next.‖

Task Chunking with parLapply

Now that we've discussed and compared clusterApply() and clusterApplyLB(), let's consider parLapply(), a third parallel lapply() function that has the same arguments and basic behavior as clusterApply() and clusterApplyLB(). But there is an important difference that makes it perhaps the most generally useful of the three.

‖ It's also possible that the extra overhead in clusterApplyLB() to determine which worker is ready for the next task could make clusterApply() more efficient in some case, but I'm skeptical.

parLapply() is a *high-level* snow function, that is actually a deceptively simple function wrapping an invocation of clusterApply():

```
> parLapply
function (cl, x, fun, ...)
docall(c, clusterApply(cl, splitList(x, length(cl)), lapply, fun, ...))
<environment: namespace:snow>
```

Basically, parLapply() splits up x into a list of subvectors, and processes those subvectors on the cluster workers using lapply(). In effect, it is *prescheduling* the work by dividing the tasks into as many chunks as there are workers in the cluster. This is functionally equivalent to using clusterApply() directly, but it can be much more efficient, since there are fewer I/O operations between the master and the workers. If the length of x is already equal to the number of workers, then parLapply() has no advantage. But if you're parallelizing an R script that already uses lapply(), the length of x is often very large, and at any rate is completely unrelated to the number of workers in your cluster. In that case, parLapply() is a better parallel version of lapply() than clusterApply().

One way to think about it is that parLapply() interprets the x argument differently than clusterApply(). clusterApply() is *low-level*, and treats x as a specification of the tasks to execute on the cluster workers using fun. parLapply() treats x as a source of disjoint input arguments to execute on the cluster workers using lapply() and fun. cluster Apply() gives you more control over what gets sent to who, while parLapply() provides a convenient way to efficiently divide the work among the cluster workers.

An interesting consequence of parLapply()'s work scheduling is that it is much more efficient than clusterApply() if you have many more tasks than workers, and one or more large, additional arguments to pass to parLapply(). In that case, the additional arguments are sent to each worker only once, rather than possibly many times. Let's try doing that, using a slightly altered parallel sleep function that takes a matrix as an argument:

```
bigsleep <- function(sleeptime, mat) Sys.sleep(sleeptime)
bigmatrix <- matrix(0, 2000, 2000)
sleeptime <- rep(1, 100)
```

I defined the sleeptimes to be small, many, and equally sized. This will accentuate the performance differences between clusterApply() and parLapply():

```
tm <- snow.time(clusterApply(cl, sleeptime, bigsleep, bigmatrix))
plot(tm)
```

Cluster Usage

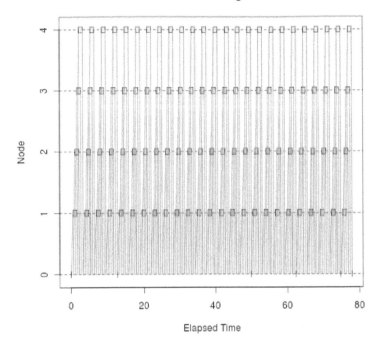

This doesn't look very efficient: you can see that there are many sends and receives between the master and the workers, resulting in relatively big gaps between the compute operations on the cluster workers. The gaps aren't due to load imbalance as we saw before: they're due to I/O time. We're now spending a significant fraction of the elapsed time sending data to the workers, so instead of the ideal elapsed time of 25 seconds,[#] it's taking 77.9 seconds.

Now let's do the same thing using parLapply():

```
tm <- snow.time(parLapply(cl, sleeptime, bigsleep, bigmatrix))
plot(tm)
```

[#]The ideal elapsed time is sum(sleeptime) / length(cl).

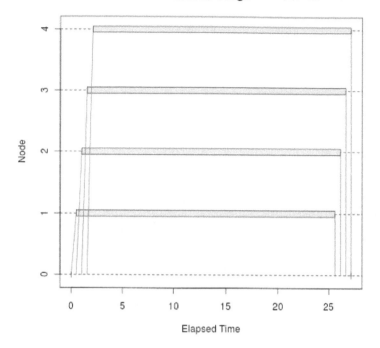

Cluster Usage

The difference is dramatic, both visually and in elapsed time: it took only 27.2 seconds, beating `clusterApply()` by 50.7 seconds.

Keep in mind that this particular use of `clusterApply()` is bad: it is needlessly sending the matrix to the worker with every task. There are various ways to fix that, and using `parLapply()` happens to work well in this case. On the other hand, if you're sending huge objects in x, then there's not much you can do, and `parLapply()` isn't going to help. My point is that `parLapply()` schedules work in a useful and efficient way, making it probably the single most useful parallel execution function in snow. When in doubt, use `parLapply()`.

Vectorizing with clusterSplit

In the previous section I showed you how `parLapply()` uses `clusterApply()` to implement a parallel operation that solves a certain class of parallel program quite nicely. Recall that `parLapply()` executes a user-supplied function for each element of x just like `clusterApply()`. But what if we want the function to operate on subvectors of x? That's similar to what `parLapply()` does, but is a bit easier to implement, since it doesn't need to use `lapply()` to call the user's function.

We could use the `splitList()` function, like `parLapply()` does, but that is a snow internal function. Instead, we'll use the `clusterSplit()` function which is very similar, and slightly more convenient. Let's try splitting the sequence from 1 to 30 for our cluster using `clusterSplit()`:

```
> clusterSplit(cl, 1:30)
[[1]]
[1] 1 2 3 4 5 6 7 8

[[2]]
[1]  9 10 11 12 13 14 15

[[3]]
[1] 16 17 18 19 20 21 22

[[4]]
[1] 23 24 25 26 27 28 29 30
```

Since our cluster has four workers, it splits the sequence into a list of four nearly equal length vectors, which is just what we need.

Now let's define `parVapply()` to split x using `clusterSplit()`, execute the user function on each of the pieces using `clusterApply()`, and combine the results using `do.call()` and `c()`:

```
parVapply <- function(cl, x, fun, ...) {
  do.call("c", clusterApply(cl, clusterSplit(cl, x), fun, ...))
}
```

Like `parLapply()`, `parVapply()` always issues the same number of tasks as workers. But unlike `parLapply()`, the user-supplied function is only executed once per worker. Let's use `parVapply()` to compute the cube root of numbers from 1 to 10 using the ^ function:

```
> parVapply(cl, 1:10, "^", 1/3)
 [1] 1.000000 1.259921 1.442250 1.587401 1.709976 1.817121 1.912931 2.000000
 [9] 2.080084 2.154435
```

This works because the ^ function takes a vector as its first argument and returns a vector of the same length.[*]

 This technique can be a useful for executing vector functions in parallel. It may also be more efficient than using `parLapply()`, for example, but for any function worth executing in parallel, the difference in efficiency is likely to be small. And remember that most, if not all, vector functions execute so quickly that it is never worth it to execute them in parallel with snow. Such fine-grained problems fall much more into the domain of multithreaded computing.

---

[*] Normally the second argument to ^ can have the same length as the first, but it must be length one in this example because `parVapply()` only splits the first argument.

Load Balancing Redux

We've talked about the advantages of parLapply() over clusterApply() at some length. In particular, when there are many more tasks than cluster workers and the task objects sent to the workers are large, there can be serious performance problems with cluster Apply() that are solved by parLapply(). But what if the task execution has significant variation so that we need load balancing? clusterApplyLB() does load balancing, but would have the same performance problems as clusterApply(). We would like a load balancing equivalent to parLapply(), but there isn't one—so let's write it.[†]

In order to achieve dynamic load balancing, it helps to have a number of tasks that is at least a small integer multiple of the number of workers. That way, a long task assigned to one worker can be offset by many shorter tasks being done by other workers. If that is not the case, then the other workers will sit idle while the one worker completes the long task. parLapply() creates exactly one task per worker, which is not what we want in this case. Instead, we'll first send the function and the fixed arguments to the cluster workers using clusterCall(), which saves them in the global environment, and then send the varying argument values using clusterApplyLB(), specifying a function that will execute the user-supplied function along with the full collection of arguments.

Here are the function definitions for parLapplyLB() and the two functions that it executes on the cluster workers:

```
parLapplyLB <- function(cl, x, fun, ...) {
  clusterCall(cl, LB.init, fun, ...)
  r <- clusterApplyLB(cl, x, LB.worker)
  clusterEvalQ(cl, rm('.LB.fun', '.LB.args', pos=globalenv()))
  r
}
LB.init <- function(fun, ...) {
  assign('.LB.fun', fun, pos=globalenv())
  assign('.LB.args', list(...), pos=globalenv())
  NULL
}
LB.worker <- function(x) {
  do.call('.LB.fun', c(list(x), .LB.args))
}
```

parLapplyLB() initializes the workers using clusterCall(), executes the tasks with clusterApplyLB(), cleans up the global environment of the cluster workers with clusterEvalQ(), and finally returns the task results.

---

† A future release of snow could optimize clusterApplyLB() by not sending the function and constant arguments to the workers in every task. At that point, this example will lose any practical value that it may have.

That's all there is to implementing a simple and efficient load balancing parallel execution function. Let's compare clusterApplyLB() to parLapplyLB() using the same test function that we used to compare clusterApply() and parLapply(), starting with clusterApplyLB():

```
bigsleep <- function(sleeptime, mat) Sys.sleep(sleeptime)
bigmatrix <- matrix(0, 2000, 2000)
sleeptime <- rep(1, 100)
tm <- snow.time(clusterApplyLB(cl, sleeptime, bigsleep, bigmatrix))
plot(tm)
```

Cluster Usage

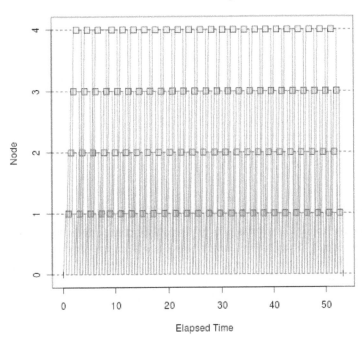

There are lots of gaps in the execution bars due to high I/O time: the master is barely able to supply the workers with tasks. Obviously this problem isn't going to scale to many more workers.

Now let's try our new parLapplyLB() function:

```
tm <- snow.time(parLapplyLB(cl, sleeptime, bigsleep, bigmatrix))
plot(tm)
```

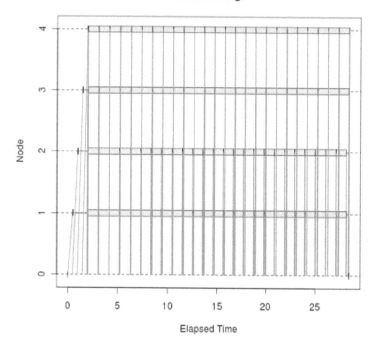

Cluster Usage

Node

Elapsed Time

That took only 28.4 seconds versus 53.2 seconds for `clusterApplyLB()`.

Notice that the first task on each worker has a short execution time, but a long *task send* time, as seen by the slope of the first four lines between the master (node 0) and the workers (nodes 1-4). Those are the worker initialization tasks executed by `cluster Call()` that send the large matrix to the workers. The tasks executed via `clusterApplyLB()` were more efficient, as seen by the vertical communication lines and the solid horizontal bars.

 By using short tasks, I was able to demonstrate a pretty noticeable difference in performance, but with longer tasks, the difference becomes less significant. In other words, we can realize decent efficiency whenever the time to compute a task significantly exceeds the time needed to send the inputs to and return the outputs from the worker evaluating the task.

Functions and Environments

 This section discusses a number of rather subtle points. An understanding of these is not essential for basic snow use, but could be invaluable when trying to debug more complicated usage scenarios. The reader may want to skim through this on a first reading, but remember to return to it if a seemingly obscure problem crops up.

Most of the parallel execution functions in snow take a function object as an argument, which I call the *worker function*, since it is sent to the cluster workers, and subsequently executed by them. In order to send it to the workers, the worker function must be serialized into a stream of bytes using the `serialize()` function.[‡] That stream of bytes is converted into a copy of the original object using the `unserialize()` function.

In addition to a list of formal arguments and a body, the worker function includes a pointer to the environment in which it was created. This environment becomes the parent of the evaluation environment when the worker function is executed, giving the worker function access to non-local variables. Obviously, this environment must be serialized along with the rest of the worker function in order for the function to work properly after being unserialized.

However, environments are serialized in a special way in R. In general, the contents are included when an environment is serialized, but not always. Name space environments are serialized by *name*, not by *value*. That is, the name of the package is written to the resulting stream of bytes, not the symbols and objects contained in the environment. When a name space is unserialized, it is reconstructed by finding and loading the corresponding package. If the package cannot be loaded, then the stream of bytes cannot be unserialized. The global environment is also serialized by name, and when it is unserialized, the resulting object is simply a reference to the existing, unmodified global environment.

So what does this mean to you as a snow programmer? Basically, you must ensure that all the variables needed to execute the worker function are available after it has been unserialized on the cluster workers. If the worker function's environment is the global environment and the worker function needs to access any variables in it, you need to send those variables to the workers explicitly. This can be done, for example, by using the `clusterExport()` function. But if the worker function was created by another function, its environment is the evaluation environment of the creator function when the worker function was created. All the variables in this environment will be serialized along with the worker function, and accessible to it when it is executed by the cluster workers. This can be a handy way of making variables available to the worker function,

---

[‡] Actually, if you specify the worker function by name, rather than by providing the definition of the function, most of the parallel execution functions (`parLapply()` is currently an exception) will use that name to look up that function in the worker processes, thus avoiding function serialization.

but if you're not careful, you could accidentally serialize large, unneeded objects along with the worker function, causing performance to suffer. Also, if you want the worker function to use any of the creator function's arguments, you need to evaluate those arguments before calling `parLapply()` or `clusterApplyLB()`; otherwise, you may not be able to evaluate them successfully on the workers due to R's lazy argument evaluation.

Let's look at a few examples to illustrate some of these issues. We'll start with a script that multiplies a vector x by a sequence of numbers:

```
a <- 1:4
x <- rnorm(4)
clusterExport(cl, "x")
mult <- function(s) s * x
parLapply(cl, a, mult)
```

In this script, the function `mult()` is defined at the top level, so its environment is the global environment.§ Thus, x isn't serialized along with `mult()`, so we need to send it to the cluster workers using the `clusterExport()` function. Of course, a more natural solution in this case would be to include x as an explicit argument to `mult()`, and then `parLapply()` would send it to the workers for us. However, using `clusterExport()` could be more efficient if we were going to reuse x by calling `mult()` many times with `parLapply()`.

Now let's turn part of this script into a function. Although this change may seem trivial, it actually changes the way `mult()` is serialized in `parLapply()`:

```
pmult <- function(cl) {
  a <- 1:4
  x <- rnorm(4)
  mult <- function(s) s * x
  parLapply(cl, a, mult)
}
pmult(cl)
```

Since `mult()` is created by `pmult()`, all of `pmult()`'s local variables will be accessible when `mult()` is executed by the cluster workers, including x. Thus, we no longer call `cluster Export()`.

`Pmult()` would be more useful if the values to be multiplied weren't hardcoded, so let's improve it by passing a and x in as arguments:

```
pmult <- function(cl, a, x) {
  x   # force x
  mult <- function(s) s * x
  parLapply(cl, a, mult)
}
scalars <- 1:4
dat <- rnorm(4)
pmult(cl, scalars, dat)
```

---

§ You can verify this with the command `environment(mult)`.

At this point, you may be wondering why x is on a line by itself with the cryptic comment "force x". Although it may look like it does nothing, this operation forces x to be evaluated by looking up the value of the variable dat (the actual argument corresponding to x that is passed to the function when pmult() is invoked) in the caller's execution environment. R uses lazy argument evaluation, and since x is now an argument, we have to force its evaluation before calling parLapply(); otherwise, the workers will report that dat wasn't found, since they don't have access to the environment where dat is defined. Note that they wouldn't say x wasn't found: they would find x, but wouldn't be able to evaluate it because they don't have access to dat. By evaluating x before calling parLapply(), mult()'s environment will be serialized with x set to the value of dat, rather than the symbol dat.

Notice in this last example that, in addition to x, a and cl are also serialized along with mult(). mult() doesn't need to access them, but since they are defined in pmult's evaluation environment, they will be serialized along with mult(). To prevent that, we can reset the environment of mult() to the global environment and pass x to mult() explicitly:

```
pmult <- function(cl, a, x) {
  mult <- function(s, x) s * x
  environment(mult) <- .GlobalEnv
  parLapply(cl, a, mult, x)
}
scalars <- 1:4
dat <- rnorm(4)
pmult(cl, scalars, dat)
```

Of course, another way to achieve the same result is to create mult() at the top level of the script so that mult() is associated with the global environment in the first place.

Unfortunately, you run into some tricky issues when sending function objects over the network. You may conclude that you don't want to use the worker function's environment to send data to your cluster workers, and that's a perfectly reasonable position. But hopefully you now understand the issues well enough to figure out what methods work best for you.

Random Number Generation

As I mentioned previously, snow is very useful for performing Monte Carlo simulations, bootstrapping, and other operations that depend on the use of random numbers. When running such operations in parallel, it's important that the cluster workers generate different random numbers; otherwise, the workers may all replicate each other's results, defeating the purpose of executing in parallel. Rather than using ad-hoc schemes for seeding the workers differently, it is better to use a parallel random number generator package. snow provides support for the rlecuyer and rsprng packages, both of which are available on CRAN. With one of these packages installed on all the nodes of your cluster, you can configure your cluster workers to use it via the clusterSetupRNG()

function. The `type` argument specifies which generator to use. To use `rlecuyer`, set `type` to `RNGstream`:

```
clusterSetupRNG(cl, type='RNGstream')
```

To use `rsprng`, set `type` to `SPRNG`:

```
clusterSetupRNG(cl, type='SPRNG')
```

You can specify a seed using the `seed` argument. `rsprng` uses a single integer for the seed, while `rlecuyer` uses a vector of six integers:

```
clusterSetupRNG(cl, type='RNGstream', seed=c(1,22,333,444,55,6))
```

 When using `rsprng`, a random seed is used by default, but not with `rlecuyer`. If you want to use a random seed with `rlecuyer`, you'll have to specify it explicitly using the seed argument.

Now the standard random number functions will use the specified parallel random number generator:

```
> unlist(clusterEvalQ(cl, rnorm(1)))
[1] -1.0452398 -0.3579839 -0.5549331  0.7823642
```

If you reinitialize the cluster workers using the same seed, you will get the same random number from each of the workers.

We can also get reproducible results using `clusterApply()`, but not with `clusterApplyLB()` because `clusterApply()` always uses the same task scheduling, while `clusterApplyLB()` does not.‖

snow Configuration

`snow` includes a number of configuration options for controlling the way the cluster is created. These options can be specified as named arguments to the cluster creation function (`makeCluster()`, `makeSOCKcluster()`, `makeMPIcluster()`, etc.). For example, here is the way to specify an alternate hostname for the master:

```
cl <- makeCluster(3, type="SOCK", master="192.168.1.100")
```

 The default value of `master` is computed as `Sys.info()[['nodename']]`. However, there's no guarantee that the workers will all be able to resolve that name to an IP address. By setting `master` to an appropriate dot-separated IP address, you can often avoid hostname resolution problems.

‖ Actually, you can achieve reproducibility with `clusterApplyLB()` by setting the seed to a task specific value. This can be done by adding the operation to the beginning of the worker function, or if using a function from a library, wrapping that function in a new function that sets the seed and then calls the library function.

You can also use the `setDefaultClusterOptions()` function to change a default configuration option during an R session. By default, the `outfile` option is set to `/dev/null`, which causes all worker output to be redirected to the null device (the proverbial bit bucket). To prevent output from being redirected, you can change the default value of `outfile` to the empty string:

```
setDefaultClusterOptions(outfile="")
```

This is a useful debugging technique which we will discuss more in "Troubleshooting snow Programs" on page 33.

Here is a summary of all of the `snow` configuration options:

Table 2-1. snow configuration options

Name	Type	Description	Default value
port	Integer	Port that the master listens on	10187
timeout	Integer	Socket timeout in seconds	31536000 (one year in seconds)
master	String	Master's hostname that workers connect to	Sys.info()["nodename"]
homogeneous	Logical	Are workers homogeneous?	TRUE if R_SNOW_LIB set, else FALSE
type	String	Type of cluster makeCluster should create	NULL, which is handled specially
outfile	String	Worker log file	"/dev/null" "nul:" on Windows
rhome	String	Home of R installation, used to locate R executable	$R_HOME
user	String	User for remote execution	Sys.info()["user"]
rshcmd	String	Remote execution command	"ssh"
rlibs	String	Location of R packages	$R_LIBS
scriptdir	String	Location of snow worker scripts	snow installation directory
rprog	String	Path of R executable	$R_HOME/bin/R
snowlib	String	Path of "library" where snow is installed	directory in which snow is installed
rscript	String	Path of Rscript command	$R_HOME/bin/Rscript $R_HOME/bin/Rscript.exe on Windows
useRscript	Logical	Should workers be started using Rscript command?	TRUE if file specified by Rscript exists
manual	Logical	Should workers be started manually?	FALSE

It is possible, although a bit tricky, to configure different workers differently. I've done this when running a `snow` program in parallel on an ad-hoc collection of workstations. In fact, there are two mechanisms available for that with the socket transport. The first approach works for all the transports. You set the `homogeneous` option to `FALSE`, which causes `snow` to use a special startup script to launch the workers. This alternate script doesn't assume that the worker nodes are set up the same as the master node, but can look for R or Rscript in the user's PATH, for example. It also supports the use of environment variables to configure the workers, such as R_SNOW_RSCRIPT_CMD and R_SNOW_LIB to specify the path of the Rscript command and the snow installation directory. These environment variables can be set to appropriate values in the user's environment on each worker machine using the shell's start up scripts.

The second approach to heterogeneous configuration only works with the socket and nws transports. When you call makeSOCKcluster(), you specify the worker machines as a list of lists. In this case, the hostname of the worker is specified by the host element of each sublist. The other elements of the sublists are used to override the corresponding option for that worker.

Let's say we want to create a cluster with two workers: n1 and n2, but we need to log in as a different user on machine n2:

```
> workerList <- list(list(host = "n1"), list(host = "n2", user = "steve"))
> cl <- makeSOCKcluster(workerList)
> clusterEvalQ(cl, Sys.info()[["user"]])
[[1]]
[1] "weston"

[[2]]
[1] "steve"

> stopCluster(cl)
```

It can also be useful to set the outfile option differently to avoid file conflicts between workers:

```
> workerList <- list(list(host = "n1", outfile = "n1.log", user = "weston"),
+                    list(host = "n2", outfile = "n2-1.log"),
+                    list(host = "n2", outfile = "n2-2.log"))
> cl <- makeSOCKcluster(workerList, user = "steve")
> clusterEvalQ(cl, Sys.glob("*.log"))
[[1]]
[1] "n1.log"

[[2]]
[1] "n2-1.log" "n2-2.log"

[[3]]
[1] "n2-1.log" "n2-2.log"

> stopCluster(cl)
```

This also demonstrates that different methods for setting options can be used together. The machine-specific option values always take precedence.

I prefer to use my `ssh` config file to specify a different user for different hosts, but obviously that doesn't help with setting `outfile`.

Installing Rmpi

As I mentioned previously, installing `Rmpi` can be problematic because it depends on MPI being previously installed. Also, there are multiple MPI distributions, and some of the older distributions have compatibility problems with `Rmpi`. In general, Open MPI is the preferred MPI distribution. Fortunately, Open MPI is readily available for modern Linux systems. The website for the Open MPI Project is *http://www.open-mpi.org/*.

Another problem is that there isn't a binary distribution of `Rmpi` available for Windows. Thus, even if you have MPI installed on a Windows machine, you will also need to install `Rmpi` from the source distribution, which requires additional tools that may also need to be installed. For more information on installing `Rmpi` on Windows, see the documentation in the `Rmpi` package. That's beyond the scope of this book.

Installation of `Rmpi` on the Mac was quite simple on Mac OS X 10.5 and 10.6, both of which came with Open MPI, but unfortunately, Apple stopped distributing it in Mac OS X 10.7. If you're using 10.5 or 10.6, you can (hopefully) install `Rmpi` quite easily:#

```
install.packages("Rmpi")
```

If you're using Mac OS X 10.7, you'll have to install Open MPI first, and then you'll probably have to build `Rmpi` from the source distribution since the binary distribution probably won't be compatible with your installation of Open MPI. I'll discuss installing `Rmpi` from the source distribution shortly, but not Open MPI.

On Debian/Ubuntu, `Rmpi` is available in the "r-cran-rmpi" Debian package, and can be installed with `apt-get`. That's the most foolproof way to install `Rmpi` on Ubuntu, for example, since `apt-get` will automatically install a compatible version of MPI, if necessary.

For non-Debian based systems, I recommend that you install Open MPI with your local packaging tool, and then try to use `install.packages()` to install `Rmpi`. This will fail if the configuration script can't find the MPI installation. In that case you will have to download the source distribution, and install it using a command such as:

```
% R CMD INSTALL --configure-args="--with-mpi=$MPI_PATH" Rmpi_0.5-9.tar.gz
```

#It's possible that newer versions of `Rmpi` won't be built for the Mac on CRAN because it won't work on Mac OS X 10.7, but it's still available as I'm writing this in September 2011.

where the value of `MPI_PATH` is the directory containing the Open MPI `lib` and `include` directories.[*] Notice that this example uses the `--configure-args` argument to pass the `--with-mpi` argument to Rmpi's configure script. Another important configure argument is `--with-Rmpi-type`, which may need to be set to "OPENMPI", for example.

As I've said, installing `Rmpi` from source can be difficult. If you run into problems and don't want to switch to Debian/Ubuntu, your best bet is to post a question on the R project's "R-sig-hpc" mailing list. You can find it by clicking on the "Mailing Lists" link on the R project's home page.

Executing snow Programs on a Cluster with Rmpi

Throughout this chapter I've been using the socket transport because it doesn't require any additional software to install, making it the most portable snow transport. However, the MPI transport is probably the most popular, at least on clusters. Of course, most of what we've discussed is independent of the transport. The difference is mostly in how the cluster object is created and how the snow script is executed.

To create an MPI cluster object, set the `type` argument of `makeCluster()` to `MPI` or use the `makeMPIcluster()` function. If you're running interactively, you can create an MPI cluster object with four workers as follows:

```
cl <- makeCluster(4, type="MPI")
```

This is equivalent to:

```
cl <- makeMPIcluster(4)
```

This creates a *spawned cluster*, since the workers are all started by snow for you via the `mpi.comm.spawn()` function.

Notice that we don't specify which machines to use, only the number of workers. For that reason, I like to compute the worker count using the `mpi.universe.size()` function, which returns the size of the initial runtime environment.[†] Since the master process is included in that size, the worker count would be computed as `mpi.universe.size()` - 1.[‡]

We shut down an MPI cluster the same as any cluster:

```
stopCluster(cl)
```

---

[*] I use the command `locate include/mpi.h` to find this directory. On my machine, this returns `/usr/lib/openmpi/include/mpi.h`, so I set MPI_PATH to `/usr/lib/openmpi`.

[†] `mpi.universe.size()` had a bug in older versions of `Rmpi`, so you may need to upgrade to Rmpi 0.5-9.

[‡] I don't use `mpi.universe.size()` when creating an MPI cluster in an interactive session, since in that context, `mpi.universe.size()` returns 1, which would give an illegal worker count of zero.

As you can see, there isn't much to creating an MPI cluster object. You can specify configuration options, just as with a socket cluster, but basically it is very simple. However, you should be aware that the cluster workers are launched differently depending on how the R script was executed. If you're running interactively, for example, the workers will always be started on the local machine. The only way that I know of to start the workers on remote machines is to execute the R interpreter using a command such as mpirun, mpiexec, or in the case of Open MPI, orterun.

As I noted previously, you can't specify the machines on which to execute the workers with makeMPIcluster(). That is done with a separate program that comes with your MPI distribution. Open MPI comes with three utilities for executing MPI programs: orterun, mpirun, and mpiexec, but they all work in exactly the same way,§ so I will refer to orterun for the rest of this discussion.

orterun doesn't know anything about R or R scripts, so we need to use orterun to execute the R interpreter, which in turn executes the R script. Let's start by creating an R script (Example 2-1), which I'll call mpi.R.

Example 2-1. mpi.R

```
library(snow)
library(Rmpi)
cl <- makeMPIcluster(mpi.universe.size() - 1)
r <- clusterEvalQ(cl, R.version.string)
print(unlist(r))
stopCluster(cl)
mpi.quit()
```

This is very similar to our very first example, except that it loads the Rmpi package, calls makeMPIcluster() rather than makeSOCKcluster(), and calls mpi.quit() at the end. Loading Rmpi isn't strictly necessary, since calling makeMPIcluster() will automatically load Rmpi, but I like to do it explicitly. makeMPIcluster() creates the MPI cluster object, as discussed in the previous section. mpi.quit() terminates the MPI execution environment, detaches the Rmpi package, and *quits R*, so it should always go at the end of your script. This is often left out, but I believe it is good practice to call it.‖ I've gotten very stern warning messages from orterun in some cases when I failed to call mpi.quit().

To execute mpi.R using the local machine as the master, and n1, n2, n3 and n4 as the workers, we can use the command:#

```
% orterun -H localhost,n1,n2,n3,n4 -n 1 R --slave -f mpi.R
```

---

§ orterun, mpirun, and mpiexec are in fact the same program in Open MPI.

‖ You can use mpi.finalize() instead, which doesn't quit R.

The orterun command in Open MPI accepts several different arguments to specify the host list and the number of workers. It does this to be compatible with previous MPI distributions, so don't be confused if you're used to different argument names.

The -H option specifies the list of machines available for execution. By using `-n 1`, orterun will only execute the command `R --slave -f mpi.R` on the first machine in the list, which is localhost in this example. This process is the master, equivalent to the interactive R session in our previous snow examples. When the master executes `make MPIcluster(mpi.universe.size() - 1)`, four workers will be spawned. orterun will execute these workers on machines n1, n2, n3 and n4, since they are next in line to receive a process.

Those are the basics, but there are a few other issues to bear in mind. First, the master and the worker processes have their working directory set to the working directory of the process executing orterun. That's no problem for the master in our example, since the master runs on the same machine as orterun. But if there isn't a directory with the same path on any of the worker machines, you will get an error. For that reason, it is useful to work from a directory that is shared across the cluster via a network file system. That isn't necessary, however. If you specify the full path to the R script, you could use the orterun `-wdir` option to set the working directory to `/tmp`:

```
% orterun -wdir /tmp -H localhost,n1,n2,n3,n4 -n 1 R --slave -f ~/mpi.R
```

This example still assumes that R is in your search path on localhost. If it isn't, you can specify the full path of the R interpreter on localhost.

That can solve some of the orterun related problems, but snow still makes a number of assumptions about where to find things on the workers as well. See "snow Configuration" on page 26 for more information.

Executing snow Programs with a Batch Queueing System

Many cluster administrators require that all parallel programs be executed via a batch queueing system. There are different ways that this can be done, and different batch queueing systems, but I will describe a method that has been commonly used for a long time, and is supported by many batch queueing systems, such as PBS/TORQUE, SGE and LSF.

Basically you submit a shell script, and the shell script executes your R script using orterun as we described in the section "Executing snow Programs on a Cluster with Rmpi" on page 30. When you submit the shell script, you tell the batch queueing system how many nodes you want using the appropriate argument to the submit command. The shell script may need to read an environment variable to learn what nodes it can execute on, and then pass that information on to the orterun command via an argument such as `-hostfile` or `-H`.

Of course the details vary depending on the batch queueing system, MPI distribution, and cluster configuration. As an example, I'll describe how this can be done using PBS/TORQUE and Open MPI.

It's actually very simple to use PBS/TORQUE with Open MPI, since Open MPI automatically gets the list of hosts using the environment variables set by PBS/TORQUE.[*] The code in Example 2-2 simplifies the orterun command used in the script.

Example 2-2. batchmpi.sh

```
#!/bin/sh
#PBS -N SNOWMPI
#PBS -j oe
cd $PBS_O_WORKDIR
orterun -n 1 /usr/bin/R --slave -f mpi.R > mpi-$PBS_JOBID.out 2>&1
```

This script uses PBS directives to specify the name of the job, and to merge the job's standard output and standard error. It then cd's to the directory from which you submitted the job, which is helpful for finding the mpi.R script. Finally it uses orterun to execute mpi.R.

We submit batchmpi.sh using the PBS/TORQUE qsub command:

```
% qsub -q devel -l nodes=2:ppn=4 batchmpi.sh
```

This submits the shell script to the devel queue, requesting two nodes with four processors per node. The -l option is used to specify the resources needed by the job. The resource specifications vary from cluster to cluster, so talk to your cluster administrator to find out how you should specify the number of nodes and processors.

If you're using LSF or SGE, you will probably need to specify the hosts via the orterun -hostfile or -H option. For LSF, use the bsub -n option to specify the number of cores, and the LSB_HOSTS environment variable to get the allocated hosts. With SGE, use the qsub -pe option and the PE_HOSTFILE environment variable. The details are different, but the basic idea is the same.

Troubleshooting snow Programs

Unfortunately, a lot of things can go wrong when using snow. That's not really snow's fault: there's just a lot of things that have to be set up properly, and if the different cluster nodes are configured differently, snow may have trouble launching the cluster workers. It's possible to configure snow to deal with heterogeneous clusters.[†] Fortunately, if your cluster is already used for parallel computing, there's a good chance it is already set up in a clean, consistent fashion, and you won't run into any problems when using snow.

Obviously you need to have R and snow installed on all of the machines that you're attempting to use for your cluster object. You also need to have ssh servers running on all of the cluster workers if using the socket transport, for instance.

---

[*] Actually, it's possible to configure Open MPI without support for PBS/TORQUE, in which case you'll have to include the arguments -hostfile $PBS_NODEFILE when executing orterun.

[†] We discuss heterogeneous configuration in "snow Configuration" on page 26.

There are several techniques available for finding out more information about what is going wrong.

When using the socket transport, the single most useful method of troubleshooting is *manual mode*. In manual mode, you start the workers yourself, rather than having snow start them for you. That allows you to run snow jobs on a cluster that doesn't have ssh servers, for example. But there are also a few other advantages to manual mode. For one thing, it makes it easier to see error messages. Rather than searching for them in log files, they can be displayed right in your terminal session.

To enable manual mode, set the `manual` option to `TRUE` when creating the socket cluster object. I also recommend specifying `outfile=""`, which prevents output from being redirected:

```
cl <- makeCluster(2, type="SOCK", manual=TRUE, outfile="")
```

`makeCluster()` will display the command to start each of the workers. For each command, I open a new terminal window, ssh to the specified machine,‡ and cut and paste the specified command into the shell.

In many cases, you'll get an error message as soon as you execute one of these commands, and the R session will exit. In that case, you need to figure out what caused the error, and solve the problem. That may not be simple, but at least you have something better to search for than "makeCluster hangs." But very often, the error is pretty obvious, like R or snow isn't installed. Also, snow may not guess the right hostname for the workers to use to connect back to the master process. In this case, R starts up and snow runs, but nothing happens. You can use your terminal window to use various network tools (`nslookup`, `ping`) to diagnose this problem.

Let's create a socket cluster using manual mode and examine the output:

```
> cl <- makeCluster(c('n1', 'n2'), type="SOCK", manual=TRUE, outfile="")
Manually start worker on n1 with
      /usr/lib/R/bin/Rscript /usr/lib/R/site-library/snow/RSOCKnode.R
MASTER=beard PORT=10187 OUT= SNOWLIB=/usr/lib/R/site-library
```

The argument `MASTER=beard` indicates that the value of the `master` option is "beard." You can now use the `ping` command from your terminal window on n1 to see if the master is reachable from n1 by that name. Here's the kind of output that you should see:

```
n1% ping beard
PING beard (192.168.1.109) 56(84) bytes of data.
64 bytes from beard (192.168.1.109): icmp_req=1 ttl=64 time=0.020 ms
```

---

‡ If ssh fails at this point, you may have found your problem.

This demonstrates that n1 is able to resolve the name "beard," knows a network route to that IP address, can get past any firewall, and is able to get a reply from the master machine.§

But if `ping` issues the error message "ping: unknown host beard", then you have a hostname resolution problem. Setting the `master` option to a different value when creating the cluster might fix the problem. Other errors may indicate a networking problem that can be fixed by your sysadmin.

If the value of `master` seems good, you should execute the command displayed by `makeCluster()` in hopes of getting a useful error message. Note that many of these problems could occur using any `snow` transport, so running a simple `snow` test code using the socket transport and manual mode can be an effective means to ensure a good setup even if you later intend to use a different transport.

The `outfile` option in itself is also useful for troubleshooting. It allows you to redirect debug and error messages to a specified file. By default, output is redirected to `/dev/null`. I often use an empty string (`""`) to prevent any redirection, as we described previously.

Here are some additional troubleshooting tips:

- Start by running on only one machine to make sure that works
- Manually `ssh` to all of the workers from the master machine
- Set the `master` option to a value that all workers can resolve, possibly using a dot-separated IP address
- Run your job from a directory that is available on all machines
- Check if there are any firewalls that might interfere

When It Works…

`snow` is a fairly high-level package, since it doesn't focus on low-level communication operations, but on execution. It provides a useful variety of functions that support *embarrassingly parallel* computation.

---

§ Of course, just because `ping` can get past a firewall doesn't mean that `snow` can. As you can see from the manual mode output, the master process is listening on port 10187, so you may have to configure your firewall to allow connections on that port. You could try the command `telnet beard 10187` as a further test.

...And When It Doesn't

Communications difficulties: snow doesn't provide functions for explicitly communicating between the master and workers, and in fact, the workers never communicate between themselves. In order to communicate between workers, you would have to use functions in the underlying communication package. Of course, that would make your program less portable, and more complicated. A package that needed to do that would probably not use snow, but use a package like nws or Rmpi directly.

The Wrap-up

In this chapter, you got a crash course on the snow package, including some advanced topics such as running snow programs via a batch queueing system. snow is a powerful package, able to run on clusters with hundreds of nodes. But if you're more interested in running on a quad-core laptop than a supercomputer, the next chapter on the multicore package will be of particular interest to you.

multicore

multicore is a popular parallel programming package for use on multiprocessor and multicore computers. It was written by Simon Urbanek, and first released on CRAN in 2009. It immediately became popular because its clever use of the fork() system call allows it to implement a parallel lapply() operation that is even easier to use than snow's parLapply().

Unfortunately, because fork() is a Posix system call, multicore can't really be used on Windows machines.[*] Fork() can also cause problems for functions that use resources that were allocated or initialized exclusively for the master, or parent process. This is particularly a problem with graphics functions, so it isn't generally recommended to use multicore with an R GUI.[†] Nevertheless, multicore works perfectly for most R functions on Posix systems, such as Linux and Mac OS X, and its use of fork() makes it very efficient and convenient, as we'll see in this chapter.

Quick Look

Motivation: You have an R script that spends an hour executing a function using lapply() on your laptop.

Solution: Replace lapply() with the mclapply() function from the multicore package.

Good because: It's easy to install, easy to use, and makes use of hardware that you probably already own.

---

[*] An experimental attempt was made to support Windows in multicore 0.1-4 using the Windows NT/2000 Native API, but it only partially works on Windows 2000 and XP, and not at all on Vista and Windows 7.

[†] multicore 0.1-4 attempts to disable the event loop in forked processes on Mac OS X in order to support the Mac GUI for R.

How It Works

multicore is intended to run on Posix-based multiprocessor and multicore systems. This includes almost all modern Mac OS X and Linux desktop and laptop computers. It can also be used on single nodes of a Linux cluster, for example, but it doesn't support the use of multiple cluster nodes, like snow.

Since multicore is rather efficient, it can handle somewhat finer-grained parallel problems than snow, but it is still intended for coarse-grained, *embarrassingly parallel* applications. It cannot compete with multithreaded programming for performing fine-grained parallelism, such as vector operations, for example.

Since multicore runs on a single computer, it doesn't give you access to greater aggregate memory, like snow. However, since fork() only copies data when it is modified, multicore often makes more efficient use of memory on a single computer than snow can on a single computer.

Setting Up

multicore is available on CRAN, so it is installed like any other CRAN package. Much of it is written in C, but it doesn't depend on any external libraries, so building it from source is fairly easy on Posix-based systems.

Here's how I usually install multicore:

```
install.packages("multicore")
```

It may ask you which CRAN mirror to use, and then it will download and install the package.

There is no Windows binary distribution available for multicore on CRAN, so if you're using Windows 2000 or XP, and want to try the experimental Windows support, you'll have to build it from the source distribution. This requires additional software to be installed, and is beyond the scope of this book.

Once you've installed multicore, you should verify that you can load it:

```
library(multicore)
```

If that succeeds, you are ready to start using multicore.

Working with It

The mclapply Function

The most important and commonly used function in the `multicore` package is `mclapply()`, which is basically a drop-in replacement for `lapply()`. It is one of the *high-level* functions in `multicore`, the others being `pvec()`, `parallel()`, and `collect()`, which we will discuss later.

Although `mclapply()` takes some additional arguments (all prefixed with "mc."), it is essentially the same as `lapply()`. If you have an R script that spends a lot of time calling `lapply()`, it's very possible that all you will have to do to parallelize it is to load the `multicore` package and replace `lapply()` with `mclapply()`.

For example, let's write a parallel K-Means using `multicore`:

```
library(multicore)
library(MASS)
results <- mclapply(rep(25, 4), function(nstart) kmeans(Boston, 4, nstart=nstart))
i <- sapply(results, function(result) result$tot.withinss)
result <- results[[which.min(i)]]
```

This is nearly identical to the sequential, `lapply()` version of K-Means from the `snow` chapter, except that we loaded the `multicore` package and replaced `lapply()` with `mclapply()`. In particular, we didn't have to create a cluster object, and we didn't have to initialize the workers by loading the `MASS` package on each of them. This is because `mclapply()` automatically starts the workers using `fork()`. These workers inherit the functions, variables and environment of the master process, making explicit worker initialization unnecessary.

It may surprise you that `mclapply()` creates worker processes every time it is called. `snow` doesn't do that since starting workers on a cluster is often rather time consuming. However, `fork()` is relatively fast, especially since it doesn't copy process data until it needs to, a technique called *copy-on-write* which takes advantage of the operating system's virtual memory system. In addition, forking the workers every time `mclapply()` is called gives each of them a virtual copy of the master's environment right at the point that `mclapply()` is executed, so worker data is in sync with the master. Thus, you don't need to recreate the master's data and environment in the workers, as in `snow`, since `fork()` does that automatically and efficiently.

The mc.cores Option

The `mclapply()` function takes a number of optional arguments that modify its behaviour. One of the most important of these is the `mc.cores` argument which controls the number of workers that are created, which is often set equal to the number of cores on the computer. By default, `mclapply()` uses the value of `getOption("cores")`, which can be set using the standard `options()` function. If this option isn't set, `mclapply()` will detect and use the number of cores on the computer.

Let's tell `mclapply()` to start two workers using `mc.cores`:

```
> unique(unlist(mclapply(1:100, function(i) Sys.getpid(), mc.cores = 2)))
[1] 4953 4954
```

As you can see, there are only two unique PIDs in the results, indicating that exactly two processes executed all 100 tasks.

Cores or Workers?

The `mc.cores` argument may sound like it specifies the number of cores to use, but it actually specifies the number of workers to start. If `mc.cores` is set equal to the number of cores and the resulting workers are the only compute intensive processes on the machine, then they will probably each get a core to themselves, but that's up to your operating system's scheduler. It is possible to influence the Linux scheduler through the `sched_setaffinity()` system call for example, but none of the functions in `multi core` do that.

Now let's use `options()` to specify three workers:

```
> options(cores = 3)
> unique(unlist(mclapply(1:100, function(i) Sys.getpid())))
[1] 4955 4956 4957
```

This will also control the number of workers started by the `pvec()` function, which we will discuss later.

The mc.set.seed Option

Another important `mclapply()` option is `mc.set.seed`. When `mc.set.seed` is set to TRUE, `mclapply()` will seed each of the workers to a different value after they have been created, which is `mclapply()`'s default behaviour. If `mc.set.seed` is set to FALSE, `mclapply()` won't do anything with respect to the random number generator.

In general, I would recommend that you leave `mc.set.seed` set to TRUE unless you have a good reason to turn it off. The problem with setting `mc.set.seed` to FALSE is that the worker processes will inherit the state of the master's random number generator if it is set.

Let's experiment with setting `mc.set.seed` to FALSE. First, we'll generate some random numbers on the workers using `mclapply()` when the master's state is *clean*:

```
> mclapply(1:3, function(i) rnorm(3), mc.cores = 3, mc.set.seed = FALSE)
[[1]]
[1] -1.268046  0.262834  2.415977
```

```
[[2]]
[1] -0.1817228  0.6496526 -0.7741212

[[3]]
[1] -0.7378100  0.1080590 -0.5902874
```

All the values are different, so everything looks fine. But watch what happens if we generate a random number on the master, and then call mclapply() again:

```
> rnorm(1)
[1] 1.847741
> mclapply(1:3, function(i) rnorm(3), mc.cores = 3, mc.set.seed = FALSE)
[[1]]
[1]  0.6995516 -0.2436397 -0.6131929

[[2]]
[1]  0.6995516 -0.2436397 -0.6131929

[[3]]
[1]  0.6995516 -0.2436397 -0.6131929
```

Now the workers all produce identical random numbers, and they will produce the same numbers if I were to call mclapply() again!

This happens because generating any random numbers or calling set.seed() creates a variable called .Random.seed in the global environment, and its value is used to generate subsequent random numbers. Therefore, if that variable exists on the master when mclapply() is executed, all the worker processes will inherit it and produce the same stream of random numbers unless something is done to *reseed* each of the workers.

When mc.set.seed is TRUE, mclapply() will explicitly set the seed differently in each of the workers before calling the user's function. Let's try that after setting the seed in the master to make sure the workers do indeed produce different random numbers:

```
> set.seed(7777442)
> mclapply(1:3, function(i) rnorm(3), mc.cores = 3, mc.set.seed = TRUE)
[[1]]
[1] -1.0757472 -0.7850815 -0.1700620

[[2]]
[1] -0.63224810 -0.04542427  1.46662809

[[3]]
[1] -0.2067085  0.7669072  0.4032044
```

As of multicore 0.1-5, setting mc.set.seed to TRUE will cause mclapply() to execute set.seed(Sys.getpid()) in each of the workers. Thus, not only are the workers seeded differently from each other, but they are also seeded differently from the workers created by previous calls to mclapply().[‡]

[‡] Of course, Unix process IDs usually only go up to about 32767, so they will wrap around eventually, but I'll ignore that issue.

Load Balancing with mclapply

What if you want load balancing with `multicore`? By default, `mclapply()` will work like `snow`'s `parLapply()` function. That is, it preschedules the work by dividing it into as many tasks as there are cores. Sometimes that works well, even if the tasks have very different lengths. But to best balance the work performed by each of the workers, prescheduling can be turned off by setting `mc.preschedule` to `FALSE`. This makes `mclapply()` work more like `snow`'s `clusterApplyLB()` function.

Let's use the parallel sleep example to see what difference prescheduling can make:

```
> set.seed(93564990)
> sleeptime <- abs(rnorm(10, 10, 10))
> system.time(mclapply(sleeptime, Sys.sleep, mc.cores = 4))
   user  system elapsed
  0.012   0.008  64.763
> system.time(mclapply(sleeptime, Sys.sleep, mc.cores = 4, mc.preschedule = FALSE))
   user  system elapsed
  0.032   0.028  57.347
```

Unfortunately we can't easily generate performance plots, as with `snow`, but the elapsed times demonstrate that it can help to turn off prescheduling if the times to execute the aggregated tasks are different. The difference isn't as great as we demonstrated between `clusterApply()` and `clusterApplyLB()`, since prescheduling tends to smooth out the differences in the length of individual tasks, but it can still be significant.

Keep in mind that a new worker is forked for every element of the vector passed to `mclapply()` when prescheduling is turned off. That means that the performance could suffer if each call to the function is relatively short. In other words, you should probably only set `mc.preschedule` to `FALSE` if the tasks are both long and varying in length. Otherwise, it's probably a safer bet to leave prescheduling turned on.

The pvec Function

The `pvec()` function was introduced in `multicore` 0.1-4. It is a *high-level* function used to execute vector functions in parallel. Let's use it to take the cube root of a vector:

```
> x <- 1:10
> pvec(x, "^", 1/3)
 [1] 1.000000 1.259921 1.442250 1.587401 1.709976 1.817121 1.912931 2.000000
 [9] 2.080084 2.154435
```

This is like the `parVapply()` function that we developed in the `snow` chapter. In both cases, the worker function is executed on subvectors of the input vector, rather than on each element of it, making it potentially more efficient and convenient than `mcl apply()` for this case.

`pvec()` takes the same additional arguments as `mclapply()` (all prefixed with "mc.")—except for `mc.preschedule`, which isn't appropriate for `pvec()`.

Many vector functions, including ^, are not compute intensive enough to make the use of pvec() worthwhile. This example runs slower on my computers than the equivalent sequential version, regardless of the vector length.

The parallel and collect Functions

The parallel() and collect() functions are the last of the *high-level* functions in multicore, and are used together. The parallel() function creates a new process using fork() to evaluate an expression in parallel with the calling process. It returns a parallelJob object which is passed to the collect() function to retrieve the result of the computation. collect() can be called with either a single parallelJob object, or a list of parallelJob objects. It returns the corresponding results in a list, in the same order that the jobs were specified to collect() (but only if wait is TRUE, as we'll see later).

Normally, you would call parallel() multiple times, and then use collect() to retrieve all of the results. This can be useful if you want to execute several different functions in parallel, or start a job running in the background and then do something else before waiting for it to complete.

Let's use parallel() and collect() to execute three different functions in parallel. For demonstration purposes, I'll define very contrived functions that each sleep for a different period of time and then return a number that identifies them:

```
library(multicore)
fun1 <- function() {Sys.sleep(10); 1}
fun2 <- function() {Sys.sleep(5);  2}
fun3 <- function() {Sys.sleep(1);  3}
```

Let's start each of them executing using parallel(), and then wait for the results using collect():

```
> f1 <- parallel(fun1())
> f2 <- parallel(fun2())
> f3 <- parallel(fun3())
> collect(list(f1, f2, f3))
$`4862`
[1] 1

$`4863`
[1] 2

$`4864`
[1] 3
```

As you can see, the results are returned in the same order that they were specified to collect().

That is the basic way of using parallel() and collect(). You can think of parallel() as a *submit* operation, and collect() as a *wait* operation, similar to batch queueing commands.

Using collect Options

The collect() function has two options that give you more control over how it waits for jobs started via parallel(): wait and timeout. If wait is set to TRUE (the default value), then collect() waits for all of the specified jobs to finish, regardless of the value of timeout, and returns the results in a list in the same order that the jobs were specified to collect(). But if wait is set to FALSE, then collect() waits for up to timeout seconds for at least one of the jobs to finish or a process to exit, and returns the results in a list in arbitrary order, using a NULL to indicate that a process exited. If no jobs finish in that time, collect() returns a NULL.

To check for results without waiting at all, you call collect() with wait set to FALSE, and timeout set to its default value of 0. Let's do that several times, pausing after the first collect() to wait for some results:

```
> f1 <- parallel(fun1())
> f2 <- parallel(fun2())
> f3 <- parallel(fun3())
> collect(list(f1, f2, f3), wait=FALSE)
NULL ❶
> Sys.sleep(15)
> collect(list(f1, f2, f3), wait=FALSE)
[[1]] ❷
[1] 3

[[2]]
[1] 2

[[3]]
[1] 1

> collect(list(f1, f2, f3), wait=FALSE)
[[1]] ❸
NULL

[[2]]
NULL

[[3]]
NULL

> collect(list(f1, f2, f3), wait=FALSE)
NULL ❹
```

Here's what each of the four values returned by collect() indicate:

❶ No results are available and no processes have exited

❷ fun3(), fun2(), and fun1() have completed

❸ All three of the processes have exited

❹ All results have been returned and all processes have exited

The timeout argument allows you to wait a specified number of seconds for at least one result to complete or one process to exit (assuming wait is set to TRUE). Let's do that repeatedly in order to collect all of the results:

```
> f1 <- parallel(fun1())
> f2 <- parallel(fun2())
> f3 <- parallel(fun3())
> collect(list(f1, f2, f3), wait=FALSE, timeout=1000000)
[[1]]
[1] 3 ❶

> collect(list(f1, f2, f3), wait=FALSE, timeout=1000000)
[[1]]
NULL ❷

> collect(list(f1, f2, f3), wait=FALSE, timeout=1000000)
[[1]]
[1] 2 ❸

> collect(list(f1, f2, f3), wait=FALSE, timeout=1000000)
[[1]]
NULL ❹

> collect(list(f1, f2, f3), wait=FALSE, timeout=1000000)
[[1]]
[1] 1 ❺

> collect(list(f1, f2, f3), wait=FALSE, timeout=1000000)
[[1]]
NULL ❻

> collect(list(f1, f2, f3), wait=FALSE, timeout=1000000)
NULL ❼
```

Here's what each of the seven values returned by collect() indicate:

❶ fun3() has completed

❷ The process that executed fun3() has exited

❸ fun2() has completed

❹ the process that executed fun2() has exited

❺ fun1() has completed

❻ The process that executed fun1() has exited

❼ All results have been returned and all processes exited

Note that if we had used a shorter timeout, such a 2, collect() would have returned some NULLs, indicating that the timeout had expired before any jobs completed or processes exited.

Parallel Random Number Generation

Unfortunately, there is no support built into the `multicore` package for any of the parallel random number generation packages, such as `rlecuyer` or `rsprng`.§ It isn't too hard to use them directly, but since the *high-level* functions fork the workers each time they are called, you can't initialize the workers once and then use them repeatedly, as in snow. You might need to generate a new seed every time you do a parallel operation, or perhaps have the workers return their state along with the result so that the next set of workers can pick up where the previous set left off.

Here's the idea: initialize each of the workers to use parallel random numbers at the start of the task. We can even use the `initSprngNode()` function which is defined in snow to do that:

```
> library(snow)
> nw <- 3
> seed <- 7777442
> kind <- 0
> para <- 0
> f1 <- parallel({
+     initSprngNode(0, nw, seed, kind, para)
+     rnorm(1)
+ })
> f2 <- parallel({
+     initSprngNode(1, nw, seed, kind, para)
+     rnorm(1)
+ })
> f3 <- parallel({
+     initSprngNode(2, nw, seed, kind, para)
+     rnorm(1)
+ })
> unlist(collect(list(f1, f2, f3)), use.names = FALSE)
[1] -0.1447636  1.0686927 -0.4137106
```

Since `parallel()` takes an expression, it is easy to prepend a call to `initSprngNode` to the expression using curly braces. We could do something similar with `mclapply()` using a wrapper function, except having an additional *varying* argument might require a bit of work. Being able to easily specify a different first argument to `initSprngNode` for each worker can make `parallel()` easier to use.

Notice that we get the same results using snow:

```
> cl <- makeCluster(3, type = "SOCK")
> seed <- 7777442
> clusterSetupSPRNG(cl, seed = seed)
> unlist(clusterEvalQ(cl, rnorm(1)), use.names = FALSE)
[1] -0.1447636  1.0686927 -0.4137106
> stopCluster(cl)
```

---

§ This is one of the problems solved by the new `parallel` package.

The same basic approach can be used with the rlecuyer package. See the source for clusterSetupRNGstream() in snow to figure out how.

The Low-Level API

So far, we've only discussed multicore's *high-level* API. There is also a low-level API which includes functions such as fork(), selectChildren(), readChild(), sendMaster(), and exit(). Those are the basic functions used to implement mclapply(), and to demonstrate how they can be used, I will implement a stripped down version of mclapply(), which I call *mclapply.init*. To make it more interesting, I will include an option called mc.init that can be used to initialize the worker processes. The value of mc.init should be a function that takes two arguments: id and cores. This function will be called in each of the child/worker processes before executing the worker function.

Here is the definition of *mclapply.init* using multicore's low-level API:

```
mclapply.init <- function(X, FUN, ..., mc.cores=4, mc.init=NULL) {
  cores <- max(min(mc.cores, length(X)), 1)
  ix <- lapply(1:cores, function(i) seq(i, length(X), by=cores))
  forkloop <- function(core) {
    proc <- fork()
    if (inherits(proc, "masterProcess")) {
      sendMaster(tryCatch({
        suppressWarnings(rm(".Random.seed", pos=.GlobalEnv))
        if (is.function(mc.init))
          mc.init(core, cores)
        lapply(X[ix[[core]]], FUN, ...)
      },
      error=function(e) {
        lapply(ix[[core]], function(i) e)
      }))
      exit(0)
    }
    proc$pid
  }
  pids <- sapply(1:cores, forkloop)
  results <- vector("list", length(X))
  while (! is.null(ready <- selectChildren(pids, 1))) {
    if (is.integer(ready)) {
      for (pid in ready) {
        data <- readChild(pid)
        if (is.raw(data)) {
          core <- which(pid == pids)
          results[ix[[core]]] <- unserialize(data)
        }
      }
    }
  }
  names(results) <- names(X)
  results
}
```

If you're familiar with Unix system programming, this should look pretty familiar. The master process calls fork() to start each worker process. Fork() returns a process object which will be a childProcess object in the parent process and a masterProcess object in the child process. The code immediately after fork() uses this process object to determine its own identity. If the object is a masterProcess, then it is the child; otherwise, it is the parent/master. The master simply returns the child's process ID contained in the childProcess object. The child executes the worker function on its portion of the input vector, and sends the result to the master process via the sendMaster() function. Meanwhile, the master calls selectChildren() to wait for the children to do something. selectChildren() returns an integer vector of process IDs of the children that have either sent data to the master or exited. The master then calls readChild() for each of those process IDs. If readChild() returns a raw vector, the master unserializes it and saves the results in a list; otherwise, it ignores the value which indicates that the child has exited.

However, I glossed over a couple of important things that the child process does before executing the worker function. First, it removes the .Random.seed variable from the global environment, in order to avoid inheriting the state of the master's random number generator. Then it calls the function specified by the mc.init argument, passing it the values of core and cores. This function can be used to initialize the worker, and the two argument values may be helpful in doing that.

Let's say that we would like the worker function to tag each of the result values with its own ID. It can do that by passing a function to mc.init that assigns the value of id to a variable in the global environment:

```
> set.worker.id <- function(id, cores) {
+     assign(".MC.WORKER.ID", id, pos = .GlobalEnv)
+ }
> mclapply.init(11:13, function(i) c(i, .MC.WORKER.ID), mc.cores = 2,
+     mc.init = set.worker.id)
[[1]]
[1] 11  1

[[2]]
[1] 12  2

[[3]]
[1] 13  1
```

Now the producer of each of the results can be identified.

Another possible use of mc.init is to initialize the random number generator. To make mclapply.init() work like mclapply() with mc.set.seed set to TRUE, we can specify the following mc.init function:

```
> set.worker.seed <- function(id, cores) {
+     set.seed(Sys.getpid())
+ }
> mclapply.init(1:3, function(i) rnorm(1), mc.init = set.worker.seed)
```

```
[[1]]
[1] 0.1699496

[[2]]
[1] 0.1616656

[[3]]
[1] -0.3883378
```

We could also initialize the workers to use a parallel random number generator package, but I'll leave that as an exercise for the reader.

When It Works...

The best feature in `multicore` is its drop-in replacement for `lapply()`: `mclapply()`.‖ It's about as close as it comes to something that "Just Works" in the world of Parallel R.#

...And When It Doesn't

The biggest gotchas in `multicore` are not supporting Windows and weak support for parallel random number generation.

The Wrap-up

You now know how to run your R scripts in parallel on the multicore computer that you probably use to read your email every day. You've also seen how running on a single machine bypasses many of the difficulties associated with running on multiple machines. So why don't more R packages take advantage of `multicore` to run in parallel? The next chapter discusses a new parallel programming package that will come built into R, starting with R 2.14.0, which might encourage more R developers to parallelize their packages. And it will be easy for you to learn, since it uses much of the code from the `snow` and `multicore` packages, so almost everything that you've learned so far will work in the new `parallel` package.

‖ If you're using `lapply()` with a function that modifies a variable outside of its local scope, then `mclapply()` probably won't work the same way as `lapply()`. However, that hasn't been a problem in my experience. Programmers tend to use for-loops for that sort of code.

\# And did I mention that `multicore` is easy to install?

parallel

A new parallel programming package named `parallel` will be included in R 2.14.0, tentatively scheduled for release on October 31, 2011. It is derived from the snow and `multicore` packages, providing many of the same functions as those packages. Some of the functions derived from `multicore` have been renamed by adding the prefix "mc.", and some of the arguments to `mclapply()` have been changed a bit, but if you have read the snow and `multicore` chapters of this book, you will have very little difficulty learning to use `parallel`.

This is an exciting development, since it makes parallel computing in R more mainstream. Hopefully the `parallel` package will be used from other standard packages, giving many more users the benefit of parallel computing, perhaps without knowing that they're using it.*

An important feature of `parallel` is its integration with the new *L'Ecuyer-CMRG* random number generator (RNG), also new in R 2.14.0. The seed of this generator can be easily advanced a given number of steps, making it very useful as a parallel RNG. This is accomplished using the same concepts used in the `rlecuyer` package, but it is a completely new implementation, so `parallel` has no dependency on the `rlecuyer` package itself.

In particular, the `multicore` derived functions in `parallel` now have true parallel RNG support, solving the biggest "gotcha" in the `multicore` package.

 This chapter was written using an experimental version of the `paral lel` package using the development version of R 2.14.0. Officially, anything in the package can change or be removed without notice until October 2011, which is just after the "all-in" date for this book. However, this is such an important package for parallel computing with R that I really wanted to include it in this book.

---

* This has already been done to a degree with multithreaded math libraries, but this takes another important step forward.

Quick Look

Motivation: You have an R script that spends two days executing a function using `lapply()` on your laptop.

Solution: Replace `lapply()` with the `mclapply()` function from the `multicore` package, and consider using `parLapply()` if you have a cluster handy.

Good because: It comes built it as of R 2.14.0, and there isn't much to learn if you've used `snow` or `multicore` before.

How It Works

 Since the `parallel` package has so much in common with the `snow` and `multicore` packages, I don't want to repeat all of the material that I just covered in the last two chapters. Instead, I assume that you've either read the `snow` and `multicore` chapters of this book, or are already reasonably familiar with those packages.

`parallel` can be used to run on Posix-based multicore systems using functions such as `mclapply()` and `mcparallel()` that were derived from the `multicore` package. But `parallel` can also be used with a "PSOCK" cluster and functions such as `parLapply()` and `clusterApplyLB()` to execute on multicore Windows systems, as well as Linux clusters. It can also be used with cluster objects that were created using `snow`, making it possible to use `parallel` with MPI as the transport.

In other words, it addresses essentially everything addressed by the `snow` and `multicore` packages.

Setting Up

This is the real beauty of `parallel`. If you're using R 2.14.0 or later, it's already installed: you don't need to install any additional packages unless you want to use the MPI, PVM, or NetWorkSpaces transports.

If you have any doubts, you can try loading it:

```
library(parallel)
```

If this fails, you should check the version of R that you're using with:

```
R.version.string
```

You need to have R 2.14.0 or better to use `parallel`.

Working with It

Getting Started

If you're using a Posix-based system, such as Linux or Mac OS X, you can use the multicore derived functions, such as mclapply(). Mclapply is basically the same as the version in the multicore package, except that a couple of the arguments work slightly differently. For example, the mc.cores argument doesn't automatically detect the number of cores in the machine. However, the parallel package does include a function to do that, called detectCores().[†]

Here's the parallel K-Means example for the parallel package using mclapply(). It is very similar to the version in the multicore chapter, except that it loads parallel, uses detectCores() to specify the value of the mc.cores argument, and uses the parallel RNG as a bonus:

```
library(parallel)
library(MASS)
RNGkind("L'Ecuyer-CMRG")
mc.cores <- detectCores()
results <- mclapply(rep(25, 4),
                    function(nstart) kmeans(Boston, 4, nstart=nstart),
                    mc.cores=mc.cores)
i <- sapply(results, function(result) result$tot.withinss)
result <- results[[which.min(i)]]
```

We'll discuss the use of RNGkind("L'Ecuyer-CMRG") in "Parallel Random Number Generation" on page 55.

The default value of the mc.cores argument is getOption("mc.cores", 2L),[‡] so you might want to add the following line to the beginning of your scripts when converting from multicore to parallel:

```
options(mc.cores=detectCores())
```

Then mclapply() and pvec() will work more like that do in multicore.

If you're using Windows, you need to use the snow derived API in parallel. The following parallel K-Means example works on any platform supported by the parallel package:

```
library(parallel)
cl <- makeCluster(detectCores())
clusterSetRNGStream(cl)
clusterEvalQ(cl, library(MASS))
results <- clusterApply(cl, rep(25, 4), function(nstart) kmeans(Boston, 4,
    nstart=nstart))
```

[†] The detectCores() function is in the multicore package, but as of version 0.1-5, is not exported.

[‡] The multicore version of mclapply() uses the option cores. This is another case where parallel adds the "mc." prefix.

```
i <- sapply(results, function(result) result$tot.withinss)
result <- results[[which.min(i)]]
stopCluster(cl)
```

This is very similar to the K-Means example in the snow chapter. The difference is in loading parallel, creating the cluster object, and enabling parallel random number generation. As with snow, we use the makeCluster() function, but in parallel, the type argument doesn't need to be specified. We'll discuss the parallel version of makeCluster() in more depth in the next section, and parallel random number generation in "Parallel Random Number Generation" on page 55.

Creating Clusters with makeCluster

If you're running on Windows or a Linux cluster, you can't use multicore derived functions such as mclapply() and pvec(). Instead you'll need to use snow derived functions such as parLapply() and clusterApplyLB(). The first argument to these functions is a cluster object, so before you can use one of these functions, you'll have to create a cluster object.

The parallel package comes with two transports: "PSOCK" and "FORK". The "PSOCK" transport is a streamlined version of snow's "SOCK" transport. It starts workers using the Rscript command, and communicates between the master and workers using socket connections.

As in snow, the makeCluster() function creates a cluster object. The default value of the type argument is "PSOCK", so we can create a "PSOCK" cluster with four local workers using the command:

```
cl <- makeCluster(4)
```

It's often useful to specify the cluster size using the detectCores() function:

```
cl <- makeCluster(detectCores())
```

If you have ssh installed, you can specify a list of machines for the first argument:

```
cl <- makeCluster(c("n1", "n2", "n3", "n4"))
```

Note that this is nearly identical to the way that socket clusters are created in snow, except that we never need to specify the type argument.

The "FORK" transport starts workers using the mcfork() function, and communicates between the master and workers using socket connections.

To create a "FORK" cluster, use makeCluster() with type set to "FORK":

```
cl <- makeCluster(4, type="FORK")
```

You cannot start workers on remote machines with a "FORK" cluster, since mcfork() is built on the fork() system call, which only creates processes on the local machine. Also, "FORK" clusters are only supported on Posix-based systems, not Windows, since fork() is a Posix system call.

An interesting feature of "FORK" clusters is that the workers inherit the data and environment of the master process. This is like the workers that are automatically started by mclapply(), but unlike the workers started in a "PSOCK" cluster. That can be useful, but it's important to remember that a "FORK" cluster is persistent, like a "PSOCK" cluster, and unlike the workers started by mclapply(). Thus, variables created on the master after creating the "FORK" cluster will not magically appear on the workers, as in mclapply(). You would have to always create a new "FORK" cluster immediately before calling parLapply(), for example, to emulate the behaviour of mclapply(). But since that won't work with any other type of cluster object, you should probably just use mclapply().

Since "FORK" clusters can be created quickly, they can be useful when parallelizing lapply() operations that are deep in some package, but you don't want to use a global variable or add an argument to dozens of functions in order to pass the cluster object to the appropriate function. In that case, you can just create the cluster object right where you need it, and shut it down afterwards. Here's one way that you could create and use a *one shot* cluster object with **parallel** that would be about as fast as using mclapply() on a Posix-based system, but would also work on Windows:

```
type <- if (exists("mcfork", mode="function")) "FORK" else "PSOCK"
cores <- getOption("mc.cores", detectCores())
cl <- makeCluster(cores, type=type)
results <- parLapply(cl, 1:100, sqrt)
stopCluster(cl)
```

Of course, you could also use mclapply() instead of a "FORK" cluster if you prefer.

Parallel Random Number Generation

The parallel random number generation support is perhaps the most interesting and important feature of **parallel**. It uses the ideas of the **rlecuyer** package, but not the code.

To use this new support in the multicore derived functions, simply set the random number generator to "L'Ecuyer-CMRG" using the RNGkind() function, and leave mc.set.seed to TRUE:

```
RNGkind("L'Ecuyer-CMRG")
mclapply(1:2, function(i) rnorm(1))
```

The first time that one of the multicore derived, high-level functions is called, the parallel random number generator is initialized. Each worker that is started by any high-level function will get a new random number stream. If the mc.reset.stream() function is called, the parallel random number generator is reinitialized using the current seed on the master.

At the time of this writing, during the development of `parallel`, `mc.reset.stream()` does not reset the state of the RNG to the same state as the first time that a high-level function is called. That may change by the time R 2.14.0 is released.

Here's one way to use `mc.reset.stream()` to get reproducible random numbers from two calls to `mclapply()`:§

```
> RNGkind("L'Ecuyer-CMRG")
> set.seed(7777442)
> mc.reset.stream()
> unlist(mclapply(1:2, function(i) rnorm(1)))
[1] -2.0043112  0.9315424
> set.seed(7777442)
> mc.reset.stream()
> unlist(mclapply(1:2, function(i) rnorm(1)))
[1] -2.0043112  0.9315424
```

Note that the second call to `set.seed()` is not technically necessary in this case, since the state of the master's RNG hasn't changed. It would be necessary if any random numbers were generated on the master between the two calls to `mc.reset.stream()`.

If `RNGkind("L'Ecuyer-CMRG")` isn't called on the master and `mc.set.seed` is `TRUE`, the workers will be randomly seeded after they are started since `.Random.seed` will be removed from the global environment if it exists. Thus, as long as you don't set `mc.set.seed` to `FALSE`, your workers should generate different random numbers, but using `L'Ecuyer-CMRG` for true parallel RNG support is recommended.

As with `multicore`, I wouldn't recommend setting `mc.set.seed` to `FALSE` unless you're sure you know what you're doing.

To use the new parallel RNG support in the `snow` derived functions, use the new `clusterSetRNGStream()` function. This replaces the `clusterSetupRNGstream()` function in `snow`:

```
> cl <- makeCluster(4, type = "FORK")
> clusterSetRNGStream(cl, 7777442)
> unlist(clusterEvalQ(cl, rnorm(1)))
[1] -0.9360073 -2.0043112  0.9315424 -0.8751129
> clusterSetRNGStream(cl, 7777442)
> unlist(clusterEvalQ(cl, rnorm(1)))
[1] -0.9360073 -2.0043112  0.9315424 -0.8751129
> stopCluster(cl)
```

Here the seed is specified as an argument to `clusterSetRNGStream()`, not using `set.seed()`.

---

§ Note that `mc.reset.stream()` is called before both calls to `mclapply()`. That was necessary in the development version of R leading up to R 2.14.0, because `mclapply()` moves to the next RNG stream if the RNG is already initialized. If the first `mc.reset.stream()` was skipped, the second `mclapply()` would use a different set of streams than the first. That may be changed in R 2.14.0, but this example will probably still work.

The `parallel` package also includes utility functions to easily advance the seed. The `nextRNGStream()` function advances a seed to the next *stream* of 2^{127} random numbers, and the `nextRNGSubStream()` function advances it to the next *sub-stream* of 2^{76} random numbers.

To advance the `L'Ecuyer-CMRG` RNG to the next *sub-stream*, simply reassign the `.Random.seed` variable in the global environment using `nextRNGStream()`:

```
.Random.seed <<- nextRNGSubStream(.Random.seed)
```

This will fail if `RNGkind("L'Ecuyer-CMRG")` hasn't been called, since `nextRNGSubStream()` requires a `L'Ecuyer-CMRG` seed.

How long before a worker runs out of random numbers?

Each worker gets a stream of 2^{127} random numbers. That's a lot. In my tests, generating 2^{29} random numbers with `runif()` took about 43 seconds. That means that if the worker did nothing but generate random numbers, it would take 0.86 *septillion years* before it started stealing random numbers from somebody else's stream.

And if you're concerned about running out of streams, you can probably stop worrying. Since the period of the `L'Ecuyer-CMRG` RNG is approximately 2^{191}, that will provide one stream of random numbers for about 2^{64} workers.

Summary of Differences

As of 9/26/2011, here is a summary of the differences between `parallel` and `multicore` or `snow`:

Differences from multicore

- `fork()` function renamed to `mcfork()`
- `exit()` function renamed to `mcexit()`
- `kill()` function renamed to `mckill()`
- `parallel()` function renamed to `mcparallel()`, but the name "parallel" is still exported for compatibility
- `collect()` function renamed to `mccollect()`, but the name "collect" is still exported for compatibility
- Different default value of `mc.cores` argument
- New `mc.allow.recursive` argument can prevent recursive calls to `mclapply()`
- `mc.set.seed` argument reimplemented using a real parallel RNG
- New `mc.reset.stream()` function
- `cores` option renamed to `mc.cores`

Differences from snow

- New function `clusterSetRNGStream()` initializes parallel RNG
- `setDefaultClusterOptions()` not exported
- The namespace doesn't export every defined function in the package
- `makeCluster()` supports additional types "FORK" and "PSOCK"
- New cluster options `methods` and `renice` when creating a cluster (although `renice` doesn't currently work on my Linux machine as of 9/26/2011).
- Cluster option `type` defaults to "PSOCK"
- Cluster option `port` can be set via the environment variable "R_PARALLEL_PORT"
- `snow.time()` function not included
- Timeout implemented using new `socketConnection()` `timeout` argument, which resolves obscure problem in `snow`

New functions useful in both sets of functions

- `detectCores()` function now exported
- Additional functions for parallel RNG: `nextRNGStream()`, `nextRNGSubStream()`

When It Works…

Since it includes the best features of both `snow` and `multicore`, `parallel` is a very versatile package. Its main limitation is in dealing with huge numbers of tasks and very large datasets.

…And When It Doesn't

`parallel` has basically the same gotchas as the `snow` and `multicore` packages, except that it does include support for parallel random number generation in the `multicore`-derived API, and allows recursive calls to `mclapply()` to be prevented.

The Wrap-up

The `parallel` package is an exciting new development in the world of Parallel R. Traditional parallel computing is finally becoming mainstream. But there are other new packages becoming available for R that use a newer parallel programming paradigm: *MapReduce*. The rest of this book will show you how to take advantage of many of those packages.

## CHAPTER 5

A Primer on MapReduce and Hadoop

Hadoop is an open-source framework for large-scale data storage and distributed computing, built on the MapReduce model. Doug Cutting initially created Hadoop as a component of the Nutch web crawler. It became its own project in 2006, and graduated to a top-level Apache project in 2008. During this time, Hadoop has experienced widespread adoption.

One of Hadoop's strengths is that it is a general framework, applicable to a variety of domains and programming languages. One use case, and the common thread of the book's remaining chapters, is to drive large R jobs.

This chapter explains some basics of MapReduce and Hadoop. It may feel a little out of place, as it's not specific to R; but the content is too important to hide in an appendix.

Have no fear: I don't dive into deep details here. There is a lot more to MapReduce and Hadoop than I could possibly cover in this book, let alone a chapter. I'll provide just enough guidance to set you on your way. For a more thorough exploration I encourage you to read the Google MapReduce paper mentioned in "A MapReduce Primer", as well as *Hadoop: The Definitive Guide* by Tom White (O'Reilly).

If you already have a grasp on MapReduce and Hadoop, feel free to skip to the next chapter.

Hadoop at Cruising Altitude

When people think "Apache Hadoop,"[*] they often think about churning through terabytes of input across clusters made of tens or hundreds of machines, or nodes. Logfile processing is such an oft-cited use case, in fact, that Hadoop virgins may think this is all the tool is good for. That would be an unfortunately narrow view of Hadoop's capabilities.

---

[*] *http://hadoop.apache.org/*

Plain and simple, Hadoop is a *framework for parallel processing:* decompose a problem into independent units of work, and Hadoop will distribute that work across a cluster of machines. This means you get your results back much faster than if you had run each unit of work sequentially, on a single machine. Hadoop has proven useful for extract-transform-load (ETL) work, image processing, data analysis, and more.

While Hadoop's parallel processing muscle is suitable for large amounts of data, it is equally useful for problems that involve large amounts of *computation* (sometimes known as "processor-intensive" or "CPU-intensive" work). Consider a program that, based on a handful of input values, runs for some tens of minutes or even a number of hours: if you needed to test several variations of those input values, then you would certainly benefit from a parallel solution.

Hadoop's parallelism is based on the *MapReduce model.* To understand how Hadoop can boost your R performance, then, let's first take a quick look at MapReduce.

A MapReduce Primer

The MapReduce model outlines a way to perform work across a cluster built of inexpensive, commodity machines. It was popularized by Google in a paper, "MapReduce: Simplified Data Processing on Large Clusters" by Jeffrey Dean and Sanjay Ghemawat.[†] Google built their own implementation to churn web content, but MapReduce has since been applied to other pursuits.

The name comes from the model's two phases, *Map* and *Reduce.* Consider that you start with a single mountain of input. In the Map phase, you divide that input and group the pieces into smaller, independent piles of related material. Next, in the Reduce phase, you perform some action on each pile. (This is why we describe MapReduce as a "divide-and-conquer" model.) The piles can be Reduced in parallel because they do not rely on one another.

A simplified version of a MapReduce job proceeds as follows:

Map Phase

1. Each cluster node takes a piece of the initial mountain of data and runs a Map task on each *record* (item) of input. You supply the code for the Map task.
2. The Map tasks all run in parallel, creating a *key/value pair* for each record. The key identifies the item's pile for the reduce operation. The value can be the record itself or some derivation thereof.

[†] *http://labs.google.com/papers/mapreduce.html*

The Shuffle

1. At the end of the Map phase, the machines all pool their results. Every key/value pair is assigned to a pile, based on the key. (You don't supply any code for the shuffle. All of this is taken care of for you, behind the scenes.)‡

Reduce Phase

1. The cluster machines then switch roles and run the Reduce task on each pile. You supply the code for the Reduce task, which gets the entire pile (that is, *all* of the key/value pairs for a given key) at once.

2. The Reduce task typically, but not necessarily, emits some output for each pile.

Figure 5-1 provides a visual representation of a MapReduce flow.§ Consider an input for which each line is a record of format (letter)(number), and the goal is to find the maximum value of (number) for each (letter). (The figure only shows letters A, B, and C, but you could imagine this covers all letters A through Z.) Cell (1) depicts the raw input. In cell (2), the MapReduce system feeds each record's line number and content to the Map process, which decomposes the record into a key (letter) and value (number). The Shuffle step gathers all of the values for each letter into a common bucket, and feeds each bucket to the Reduce step. In turn, the Reduce step plucks out the maximum value from the bucket. The output is a set of (letter),(maximum number) pairs.

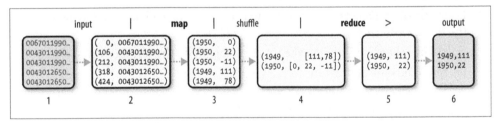

Figure 5-1. MapReduce data flow

This may still feel a little abstract. A few examples should help firm this up.

Thinking in MapReduce: Some Pseudocode Examples

Sometimes the toughest part of using Hadoop is trying to express a problem in MapReduce terms. Since the payoff—scalable, parallel processing across a farm of commodity hardware—is so great, it's often worth the extra mental muscle to convince a problem to fit the MapReduce model.

---

‡ Well, you *can* provide code to influence the shuffle phase, under certain advanced cases. Please refer to *Hadoop: The Definitive Guide* for details.

§ A hearty thanks to Tom White for letting us borrow and modify this diagram from his book.

Let's walk through some pseudocode for the Map and Reduce tasks, and how they handle key/value pairs. Note that there is a special case in which you can have a Map-only job for simple parallelization. (I'll cover real code in the next chapters, as each Hadoop-related solution I present has its own ways of talking MapReduce.)

For these examples, I'll use a fictitious text input format in which each record is a comma-separated line that describes a phone call:

```
{date},{caller num},{caller carrier},{dest num},{dest carrier},{length}
```

Calculate Average Call Length for Each Date

This uses the Map task to group the records by day, then calculates the mean (average) call length in the Reduce task.

Map task

- Receives a single line of input (that is, one input record)
- Uses text manipulation to extract the {date} and {length} fields
- Emits key: {date}, value: {length}

Reduce task

- Receives key: {date}, values: {length1 … lengthN} (that is, each reduce task receives *all* of the call lengths for a *single* date)
- Loops through {length1 … lengthN} to calculate total call length, and also to note the number of calls
- Calculates the mean (divides the total call length by the number of calls)
- Outputs the date and the mean call length

Number of Calls by Each User, on Each Date

This time, the goal is to get a breakdown of each caller for each date. The Map phase will define the keys to group the inputs, and the Reduce task will perform the calculations. Notice that the Map task emits a dummy value (the number 1) as its value because we use the Reduce task for a simple counting operation.

Map task

- Receives single line of input
- Uses text manipulation to extract {date}, {caller num}
- Emits key: {date}{caller num}, value: 1

Reduce task

- Receives key: {date}{caller num}, value: {1 … 1}
- Loops through each item, to count total number of items (calls)
- Outputs {date}, {caller num} and the number of calls

Run a Special Algorithm on Each Record

In this last case, there's no need to group the input records; we simply wish to run some special function for every input record. Because the Map phase runs in parallel across the cluster, we can leverage MapReduce to execute some (possibly long-running) code for each input record and reap the time-saving parallel execution.

Chances are, this is how you will run a good deal of your R code through Hadoop.

Map task

- Receives single line of input
- Uses text manipulation to extract function parameters
- Passes those parameters to a potentially long-running function
- Emits key: {function output}, value: {null}

(There is no Reduce task.)

Binary and Whole-File Data: SequenceFiles

Earlier, I oversimplified Hadoop processing when I explained that input records are lines of delimited text. If you expect that *all* of your input will be of this form, feel free to skip this section. You're in quite a different boat if you plan to use Hadoop with binary data (sound files, image files, proprietary data formats) or if you want to treat an entire text file (XML document) as a record.

By default, when you point Hadoop to an input file, it will assume it is a text document and treat each line as a record. There are times when this is not what you want: maybe you're performing feature extraction on sound files, or you wish to perform sentiment analysis on text documents. How do you tell Hadoop to work on the *entire* file, be it binary or text?

The answer is to use a special archive called a *SequenceFile*.[||] A SequenceFile is similar to a zip or tar file, in that it's just a container for other files. Hadoop considers each file in a SequenceFile to be its own record.

[||] There's another reason you want to use a SequenceFile, but it's not really an issue for this book. The curious among you can take a gander at Tom White's explanation in "The Small Files Problem," at *http://www .cloudera.com/blog/2009/02/the-small-files-problem/*.

To manage zip files, you use the `zip` command. Tar file? Use `tar`. SequenceFiles? Hadoop doesn't ship with any tools for this, but you still have options: you can write a Hadoop job using the Java API; or you can use the `forqlift` command-line tool. Please see the sidebar "Getting to Know forqlift" for details.

Getting to Know forqlift

`forqlift` is a command-line tool for managing SequenceFile archives. Using `forqlift`, you can:

- Create a SequenceFile from files on your local disk
- Extract data from a SequenceFile back to local disk files
- List the contents of SequenceFiles
- Convert traditional zip and tar files to and from SequenceFile format

`forqlift` strives to be simple and straightforward. For example, to create a SequenceFile from a set of MP3s, you would run:

```
forqlift create --file=/path/to/file.seq *.mp3
```

Then, in a Hadoop job, the Map task's key would be an MP3's filename and the value would be the file's contents.

A prototype `forqlift` was born of my early experiments with Hadoop and Mahout: I needed a way to quickly create and extract SequenceFiles without distracting myself from the main task at hand. Over time I polished it up, and now I provide it free and open-source to help others.

`forqlift` supports options and features beyond what I've mentioned here. For more details and to download this tool, please visit *http://www.forqlift.net/* .

No Cluster? No Problem! Look to the Clouds...

The techniques presented in the next three chapters all require that you have a Hadoop cluster at your disposal. Your company may already have one, in which case you'll want to talk to your Hadoop admins to get connection details.

If your company doesn't have a Hadoop cluster, or you're working on your own, you can build one using Amazon's cloud computing wing, Amazon Web Services (AWS).# Setting up a Hadoop cluster in the AWS cloud would merit a book on its own, so we can only provide some general guidance here. Please refer to Amazon's documentation for details.

AWS provides computing resources such as virtual servers and storage in *metered* (pay-per-use) fashion. Customers benefit from fast ramp-up time, zero commitment, and no

---

#http://aws.amazon.com/

up-front infrastructure costs compared to traditional datacenter computing. These factors make AWS especially appealing to individuals, start-ups, and small firms.

You can hand-build your cluster using virtual servers on *Elastic Compute Cloud (EC2)*, or you can leverage the Hadoop-on-demand service called *Elastic MapReduce (EMR)*.

Building on EC2 means having your own Hadoop cluster in the cloud. You get complete control over the node configuration and long-term storage in the form of HDFS, Hadoop's distributed filesystem. This comes at the expense of doing a lot more grunt work up-front and having to know more about systems administration on EC2. The Apache Whirr project* provides tools to ease the burden, but there's still no free lunch here.

By comparison, EMR is as simple and hands-off as it gets: tell AWS how many nodes you want, what size (instance type) they should be, and you're off to the races. EMR's value-add is that AWS will build the cluster for you, on-demand, and run your job. You only pay for data storage, and for machine time while the cluster is running. The trade-off is that, as of this writing, you don't get to choose which machine image (AMI) to use for the cluster nodes. Amazon deploys its own AMI, currently based on Debian 5, Hadoop 0.20.0, and R 2.7. You have (limited) avenues for customization through EMR "bootstrap action" scripts. While it's possible to upgrade R and install some packages, this gets to be a real pain because you have to do that every time you launch a cluster.

When I say "each time," I mean that an EMR-based cluster is designed to be ephemeral: by default, AWS tears down the cluster as soon as your job completes. All of the cluster nodes and resources disappear. That means you can't leverage HDFS for long-term storage. If you plan to run a series of jobs in short order, pass the `--alive` flag on cluster creation and the cluster will stay alive until you manually shut it down. Keep in mind, though, this works against one of EMR's perks: you'll continue to incur cost as long as the cluster is running, even if you forget to turn it off.

Your circumstances will tell you whether to choose EC2 or EMR. The greater your desire to customize the Hadoop cluster, the more you should consider building out a cluster on EC2. This requires more up-front work and incurs greater runtime cost, but allows you to have a true Hadoop cluster (complete with HDFS). That makes the EC2 route more suitable for a small company that has a decent budget and dedicated sysadmins for cluster administration. If you lack the time, inclination, or skill to play sysadmin, then EMR is your best bet. Sure, running bootstrap actions to update R is a pain, but it still beats the distraction of building your own EC2 cluster.

In either case, the economics of EC2 and EMR lower Hadoop's barrier to entry. One perk of a cloud-based cluster is that the return-on-investment (ROI) calculations are very different from those of a physical cluster, where you need to have a lot of Hadoop-able "big-data" work to justify the expense. By comparison, a cloud cluster opens the door to using Hadoop on "medium-data" problems.

---

* *http://incubator.apache.org/whirr/*

The Wrap-up

In this chapter, I've explained MapReduce and its implementation in Apache Hadoop. Along the way, I've given you a start on building your own Hadoop cluster in the cloud. I also oversimplified a couple of concepts so as to not drown you in detail. I'll pick up on a couple of finer points in the next chapter, when I discuss mixing Hadoop and R: I call it, quite simply, *R+Hadoop*.

## CHAPTER 6

R+Hadoop

Of the three Hadoop-related strategies we discuss in this book, this is the most raw: you get to spend time up close and personal with the system. On the one hand, that means you have to understand Hadoop. On the other hand, it gives you the most control. I'll walk you through Hadoop programming basics and then explain how to use it to run your R code.

If you skipped straight to this chapter, but you're new to Hadoop, you'll want to review Chapter 5.

Quick Look

Motivation: You need to run the same R code many times over different parameters or inputs. For example, you plan to test an algorithm over a series of historical data.

Solution: Use a Hadoop cluster to run your R code.

Good because: Hadoop distributes work across a cluster of machines. As such, using Hadoop as a driver overcomes R's single-threaded limitation as well as its memory boundaries.

How It Works

There are several ways to submit work to a cluster, two of which are relevant to R users: *streaming* and the *Java API*.

In streaming, you write your Map and Reduce operations as R scripts. (Well, streaming lets you write Map and Reduce code in pretty much any scripting language; but since this is a book about R, let's pretend that R is all that exists.) The Hadoop framework launches your R scripts at the appropriate times and communicates with them via standard input and standard output.

By comparison, when using the Java API, your Map and Reduce operations are written in Java. Your Java code, in turn, invokes `Runtime.exec()` or some equivalent to launch your R scripts.

Which is the appropriate method depends on several factors, including your understanding of Java versus R, and the particular problem you're trying to solve. Streaming tends to win for rapid development. The Java API is useful for working with binary or output input data such as images or sound files. (You can still use streaming for binary data, mind you, but it requires additional programming and infrastructure overhead. I'll explain that in detail in the code walkthroughs.)

Setting Up

You can fetch the Hadoop distribution from *http://hadoop.apache.org/*. So long as you also have a Java runtime (JRE or SDK) installed, this is all you'll need to submit work to a Hadoop cluster. Just extract the ZIP or tar file and run the `hadoop` command as we describe below.

Check with your local Hadoop admins for details on how to connect to your local cluster. If you don't have a Hadoop cluster, you can peek at Chapter 5 for some hints on how to get a cluster in the cloud.

Working with It

Let's take a walk through some examples of mixing Hadoop and R. In three cases, I'll only use the Map phase of MapReduce for simple task parallelization. In the fourth example, I'll use the full Map and Reduce to populate and operate on a `data.frame`.

The unifying theme of these examples is the need to execute a block of long-running R code for several (hundred, or thousand, or whatever) iterations. Perhaps it is a function that will run once for each of many input values, such as an analysis over each day's worth of historical data or a series of Markov Chains.[*] Maybe you're trying a variety of permutations over a function's parameter values in search of some ideal set, such as in a timeseries modeling exercise.[†] So long as each iteration is independent—that is, it does not rely on the results from any previous iteration—this is an ideal candidate for parallel execution.

Some examples will borrow the "phone records" data format mentioned in the previous chapter.

---

[*] Please note that the need for iteration independence makes Hadoop unsuitable for running a *single* Markov Chain process, since each iteration relies on the previous iteration's results. That said, Hadoop is more than suitable for running a *set* of Markov Chain processes, in which each task computes an entire Markov Chain.

[†] Some Hadoop literature refers to this type of work as a *parameter sweep*.

Simple Hadoop Streaming (All Text)

Situation: In this first example, the input data is several million lines of plain-text phone call records. Each CSV input line is of the format:

```
{date},{caller num},{caller carrier},{dest num},{dest carrier},{length}
```

The plan is to analyze each call record separately, so there's no need to sort and group the data. In turn, we won't need the full MapReduce cycle but can use a Map-only job to distribute the work throughout the cluster.

The code: To analyze each call record, consider a function `callAnalysis()` that takes all of the record's fields as parameters:

```
callAnalysis( date , caller.num, caller.carrier , dest.num , dest.carrier , length )
```

Hadoop streaming does not invoke R functions directly. You provide an R script that calls the functions, and Hadoop invokes your R script. Specifically, Hadoop will pass an entire input record to the Map operation R script via standard input. It's up to your R script to disassemble the record into its components (here, split it by commas) and feed it into the function (see Example 6-1).

Example 6-1. mapper.R

```
#! /usr/bin/env Rscript
input <- file( "stdin" , "r" )
while( TRUE ){
    currentLine <- readLines( input , n=1 )  ❶

    if( 0 == length( currentLine ) ){
        break
    }

    currentFields <- unlist( strsplit( currentLine , "," ) )  ❷

    result <- callAnalysis(
        currentFields[1] , currentFields[2] , currentFields[3] ,
        currentFields[4] , currentFields[5] , currentFields[6]
    )  ❸

    cat( result , "\n" , sep="" )  ❹
}
close( input )
```

❶ Hadoop Streaming sends input records to the Mapper script via standard input. A Map script may receive one or more input records in a single call, so we read from standard input until there's no more data.

❷ Split apart the comma-separated line, to address each field as an element of the vector `currentFields`.

❸ Send all of the fields to the `callAnalysis()` function. In a real-world scenario, this would have assigned each element of `currentFields` to a named variable. That would make for cleaner code.

❹ Here, the code assumes the return value of `callAnalysis()` is a simple string. The script sends this to standard output for Hadoop to collect.

This may not be the most efficient code. That's alright. Large-scale parallelism tends to wash away smaller code inefficiencies.

Put another way, clustered computer power is cheap compared to human thinking-power. Save your brain for solving data-related problems and let Hadoop pick up any slack. Your R code would have to be *extremely* inefficient before an extensive tuning exercise would yield a payoff.

Prototyping A Hadoop Streaming Job

It's a wise idea to test your job on your own workstation, using a subset of your input data, before sending it to the cluster for the full run. Hadoop's default "local" mode does just this.

Additionally, for streaming jobs, you can chain the scripts with pipes to simulate a workflow. For example:

```
cat input-sample.txt | ./mapper.R | sort | ./reducer.R
```

Chaining gives you a chance to iron out script-specific issues before you test with a local Hadoop job.

Running the Hadoop job:

❶
```
export HADOOP_VERSION="0.20.203.0"
export HADOOP_HOME="/opt/thirdparty/dist/hadoop-${HADOOP_VERSION}"
export HADOOP_COMMAND="${HADOOP_HOME}/bin/hadoop"
export HADOOP_STREAMING_JAR="${HADOOP_HOME}/contrib/streaming/hadoop-streaming-${HADOOP_VERSION}.jar"
export HADOOP_COMPRESSION_CODEC="org.apache.hadoop.io.compress.GzipCodec"
export HADOOP_INPUTFORMAT="org.apache.hadoop.mapred.lib.NLineInputFormat"

${HADOOP_COMMAND} jar ${HADOOP_STREAMING_JAR} \
 \
 -D mapreduce.job.reduces=0 \ ❷
 -D mapred.output.compress=true \ ❸
 -D mapred.output.compression.codec=${HADOOP_COMPRESSION_CODEC} \
 -D mapred.task.timeout=600000 \ ❹
 \
 -inputformat ${HADOOP_INPUTFORMAT} \ ❺
 -input /tmp/call-records.csv \
 -output /tmp/hadoop-out \
 -mapper $PWD/mapper.R
```

This is a pretty standard command line for Hadoop streaming: it specifies the streaming JAR, the mapper script, and the input and output locations. Note that the "generic" Hadoop options, which begin with -D, always come first.

There are a few points of note:

❶ Set some parameters as environment variables for easy reuse.

❷ Hadoop accepts configuration values on the command line, passed in using -D. (Please note that, unlike Java system properties, Hadoop expects a space between the -D and the property name.) The code disables the Reduce phase because this job uses Hadoop just for its Map-side parallelism.

❸ Compress the output. This saves space and reduces transfer time when we download the output data from HDFS (or S3, if you're using Elastic MapReduce).‡ You can also specify BZip2Codec for bzip2 compression.

❹ Hadoop will kill a task that is unresponsive; if Hadoop kills too many tasks, it will mark the entire job as failed. A streaming job's only sign of life is printing to standard output, so this line tells Hadoop to give each Map task ten minutes (600,000 milliseconds) before declaring it a goner. You may have to increase the timeout for your own jobs. I'd suggest you experiment a little to see how long a given task will run, then set the timeout to double that value so you have plenty of headroom.

❺ By default, Hadoop tries to divide your input data into sizable chunks, known as *splits*. In a typical Hadoop "big-data" scenario, this is the smart thing to do because it limits the amount of data shipped around the cluster. For "big-CPU" or "big-memory" jobs, in which each input record itself represents a sizable operation, this chunking can actually work against parallelism: it's possible that a file with several hundred records may be divided into only two splits, such that the entire job would be saddled on just two cluster nodes. When using NLineInputFormat, Hadoop treats each line as a split and spreads the work evenly throughout the cluster.

(This code works for Hadoop 0.19 and 0.20. For Hadoop 0.21, use org.apache.hadoop.mapreduce.lib.input.NLineInputFormat. Note the subtle difference in class name!)

 Resist the temptation to disable the timeout (by setting it to 0). An unresponsive task may be one that has truly hung on a particular input, or is stuck in an infinite loop. If Hadoop doesn't kill that task, how will you ever know that it's broken?

‡ By the way, if you're going to feed the output data back into R on your workstation, remember that R can natively read gzip and bzip2-compressed files.

Reviewing the output: A typical Hadoop job will create several files, one for each Reduce operation. Since this is a Map-only job, there is just one file, called /tmp/hadoop-out/part-0000.gz. You can use `gunzip` to uncompress the file and then review the contents.

Anything the script wrote to standard output would be included this output file. That is, Hadoop doesn't discern between the lines you *want* in the output (such as the output from the fictional `callAnalysis()` function) and any lingering `cat()` or `print()` calls in your code or in the modules you load. If you find stray content in your job's output, you can post-process those files or suppress the output in your code. Here, "post-process" is a fancy term for `grep`'ing the job output file to extract the lines of interest. "Suppress" means you call `sink()` to selectively disable standard output:

```
sink( "/dev/null" ) ## suppress standard output

... do the work ...

sink() ## restore standard output

cat(  ... your intended result ... )
    ... exit the script
```

Streaming, Redux: Indirectly Working with Binary Data

As of this writing, Hadoop Streaming can only be used for text input and output. (This is slated to change in a future Hadoop release.) This doesn't preclude you from *working with binary data* in a streaming job; but it does preclude your Map and Reduce scripts from *accepting binary input and producing binary output*. This example presents a workaround.

Situation: Imagine that you want to analyze a series of image files. Perhaps they are frames from a video recording, or a file full of serialized R objects, or maybe you run a large photo-sharing site. For this example, let's say you have R code that will perform image feature extraction. Each image is an independent unit of work, so assuming you have a decent number of images (and/or feature extraction takes some noticeable amount of time), a Map-only Hadoop job is a good fit.

The code: Remember, though, that Hadoop Streaming can only handle line-by-line text input and output so you have to get creative here. One option would be to feed your Hadoop Streaming job an input of *pointers* to the data, which your R script could then fetch and process locally. For example:

- Host the data on an internal web server, and feed Hadoop a list of URLs
- Ditto, but use an NFS mount
- Use `scp` to pull the files from a remote system
- Make a SQL call to a database system

(Notice that I don't mention using HDFS. Remember that HDFS doesn't work well with small files. I'll cover a different approach in the next example.)

For this example, let's say the mythical `imageFeatureExtraction()` function accepts an R `url()` connection:

```
#! /usr/bin/env Rscript
input <- file( "stdin" , "r" )
while( TRUE ){
    currentLine <- readLines( input , n=1 )

    if( 0 == length( currentLine ) ){
        break
    }

    pulledData <- url( currentLine ) )

    result <- imageFeatureExtraction( url( currentLine ) )
    cat( result , "\n" , sep="" )
}
close( input )
```

Running the Hadoop job: As far as Hadoop is concerned, this example looks just like the previous one (all the changes are in the R script), so it uses the same command line.

Reviewing the output: If your job outputs text (such as a series of numbers describing the binary data) then you can send that to standard output, as usual.

Let's say your job yields binary *output*, such as a series of charts. In that case, you can use the same idea as you did for the input, and push the output to another system:

- Copy it to an NFS mount
- Use an HTTP POST operation to send the data to a remote web server
- Call scp to ship the data to another system
- Use SQL to push the data to an RDBMS

and so on.

Caveats: Keep in mind that this method is not perfect.

A Hadoop cluster is a robust beast. Between the software-side framework and the required hardware layout, you are protected from hard disk failures, node crashes, and even loss of network connectivity.

To reap this benefit, though, the job must be self-contained from Hadoop's perspective. *Everything required for the job must exist within the cluster.* Map and Reduce scripts, input data, and output must all live in HDFS (S3 if you are using Elastic MapReduce).

Once you rely on systems or services outside of the cluster, you lose in four ways:

Loss of robustness
Hadoop can't manage a failure or crash in a remote service.

Scaling

> While the cluster may not break a sweat running your large job, that remote web server or NFS mount may fail under the weight of a Hadoop-inflicted flood of activity.

Overhead

> Any of the methods described above—SSH, web server, NFS mount—requires additional setup. If you are somehow able to get this one past your sysadmins (oh, especially that NFS one), expect them to be very unhappy with you down the line.

Idempotence/risk of side effects

> Hadoop may employ *speculative execution*. This is a fancy way of saying that, under certain circumstances, Hadoop might run a given Map or Reduce task more than once. Hadoop may kill a task in mid-run and launch it elsewhere (if it detects a timeout) or it may concurrently launch a duplicate task (if the first task seems to be taking too long to complete).

> Under pure Hadoop circumstances, when all job-related activity takes place within the cluster walls, this is not a problem because Hadoop itself takes care of retrieving the output from only one of the multiple executions of that same Map or Reduce task. But when you leverage data or services from outside the cluster, those are considered side effects of a task. Hadoop doesn't know what your Map or Reduce code is doing; it only knows how long it takes to run, and whether it meets Hadoop's criteria for success or failure. That means it's up to you to handle side effects such as duplicate submissions to that remote web server.

This may sound like a long list of caveats, but whether it's really a hurdle depends on your circumstances. Leveraging external services and side effects will work just fine if most of the "action" will take place inside Hadoop, or the external data is just a small part of the process, or multiple execution is not a problem.

That said, there is another way to handle binary data in a streaming job but still keep all the data in the cluster. It's slightly more involved than the methods described in this example, but the trade-off may be worth your while. In the next section, I'll show you how to do this using the Java API instead of Streaming.

The Java API: Binary Input and Output

Situation: You still wish to perform feature extraction on a series of image files, but you feel the previous solution is too fragile. You want the job to be self-contained, from a Hadoop perspective.

The code: Recall, from the previous chapter, that if you're processing whole-file data (text or binary) with Hadoop, you'll need to pack those files into a SequenceFile archive. The streaming API cannot presently handle SequenceFiles but the Java API can. You can use the Java API to extract data from the SequenceFile input, write it to a predictable filename, and launch an R script that operates on that file.

Once again, we need Hadoop for a one-stage parallel execution, so this will be a Map-only job.

First, let's look at the Java code in Example 6-2. Hadoop Java code is typically compiled into a JAR that has at least two classes: the *driver* that configures the job and the *mapper* that is run for a Map task. (Jobs that have a Reduce step will include a class for the Reduce task.)

Example 6-2. Excerpt from the tool class, Driver.java

```
public class Driver extends Configured implements Tool { ❶

  public int run( String[] args ) throws Exception {
    final Job job = new Job( getConf() ) ;

    job.setJobName( "Parallel R: Chapter 5, example 3" ) ;
    job.setMapperClass( Ch5Ex3Mapper.class ) ; ❷

    FileInputFormat.addInputPath( job , new Path( args[0] ) ) ; ❸
    FileOutputFormat.setOutputPath( job , new Path( args[1] ) ) ;
    job.setInputFormatClass( SequenceFileInputFormat.class ) ; ❹

    job.setOutputKeyClass( Text.class ) ; ❺
    job.setOutputValueClass( Text.class ) ;

    job.getConfiguration().setBoolean( "mapred.output.compress" , true ) ; ❻

    job.getConfiguration().setClass( "mapred.output.compression.codec" ,
      BZip2Codec.class , CompressionCodec.class ) ;
    job.getConfiguration().setInt( "mapreduce.job.reduces" , 0 ) ; ❼

    return( job.waitForCompletion( true ) ? 0 : 1 ) ;

  }
}
```

❶ Driver extends the Hadoop base class Configured and implements the interface Tool. The combined effect is that Driver gets some convenience methods for setting up the job and Hadoop will take care of parsing Hadoop-specific options for us. For example, when we launch the job based on Driver, it will magically understand any -D options passed on the Hadoop command line.

❷ Set the class that will be run for Map tasks. As this is a Map-only job, there is no need to set a class for Reduce tasks. (Technically, Hadoop defaults to using its no-op Reducer class, which simply parrots the Map phase's output.)

❸ Remember when I said that using Tool and Configured would simplify command line processing? Here, the arg[] array contains all command line elements *after* the general Hadoop options. The first one is the input path, the second is the output path.

❹ Per this line, Hadoop will expect all job input to be in SequenceFiles.

❺ The Reduce phase also emits a series of key/value pairs. These two lines tell Hadoop that both key and value will be plain-text.

❻ For streaming jobs, you set configuration properties using -D to ask Hadoop to compress the output. You can still do that on the command line with a Java-based job, or you can embed that in the Java code, as shown here.

❼ Tell Hadoop not to run any reducers.

Example 6-3. Excerpt from the Mapper class, Ch6Ex3Mapper.java

```java
public class Ch5Ex3Mapper extends Mapper<Text, BytesWritable , Text , Text> { ❶

private final Text _outputValue ;  ❷
private final StringBuilder _rOutputBuffer ;

public void map(Text inputKey , BytesWritable inputValue , Context context )
    throws IOException , InterruptedException {

    _outputValue.clear() ;  ❸
    if( _rOutputBuffer.length() > 0 ){
        _rOutputBuffer.delete( 0 , _rOutputBuffer.length() ) ;
    }

    BufferedReader rOutputReader = null ;
    OutputStream fileWriteHandle = null ;
    final File currentFile = new File( inputKey.toString() ) ;

    try{

        // write the raw bytes to a file. (input key name is the file name)
        fileWriteHandle = new FileOutputStream( currentFile ) ;  ❹
        fileWriteHandle.write( inputValue.getBytes() , 0, inputValue.getLength() ) ;
        closeOutputStream( fileWriteHandle ) ;

        final ArrayList<String> tempList = new ArrayList<String>() ;  ❺
        final List<String> commandLine = new ArrayList<String>() ;
        commandLine.add( "/usr/bin/env" ) ;
        commandLine.add( "R" ) ;
        commandLine.add( "--vanilla" ) ;
        commandLine.add( "--slave" ) ;
        commandLine.add( "--file=helper.R" ) ;
        commandLine.add( "--args " ) ;
        commandLine.add( inputKey.toString() ) ;

        final Process runtime = new ProcessBuilder( commandLine )
            .redirectErrorStream( true )
            .start() ;  ❻

        final int exitCode = runtime.waitFor() ;
        rOutputReader = new BufferedReader(
          new InputStreamReader( runtime.getInputStream() ) ) ;

        if( 0 != exitCode ){
            _rOutputBuffer.append( "error! " ) ;
```

```
        }

        _rOutputBuffer.append( rOutputReader.readLine() ) ;   ❼
        _outputValue.set( _rOutputBuffer.toString() ) ;

        context.write( inputKey , _outputValue ) ;   ❽


    }catch( final Exception rethrow ){
        throw( new IOException( rethrow ) ) ;
    }finally{
            // … close handles and delete the image file ...
    }

  }

}
```

❶ Per this class definition, the map() operation will expect a text string and binary data as the input key/value pair, and will emit text for the output key/value pair. Please note that the SequenceFile must therefore use a Text object as the key and a Byte sWritable as the value. (If you used forqlift to create your SequenceFiles, this has been done for you.)

❷ Hadoop will try to reuse a single Mapper or Reducer object several times throughout the life of a single job. As such, it's considered good form (read: more efficient) to use instance variables instead of local method variables when possible. Here, the code recycles the Text object used for the output value and also a StringBuilder that to holds the R script's output.

❸ For that same reason, the code performs some cleanup on those instance variables each time it enters map().

❹ Write the binary data to a file on-disk that R can access. This code assumes the input key is the file's name and the value is its data.

❺ Build a command line to run R. Notice that the final element is the input key, which is the name of the image file to process.

❻ This line launches R. The code uses ProcessBuilder, instead of Runtime.exec(), in order to combine the R script's standard output and standard error. That will make it easier to collect the script's output.

❼ Collect the R script's output. A successful run of helper.R yields a single line of output.R+, so that's all the code fetches. (Production-grade code would fetch all of the output and sift through it to check for problems.)

❽ Package up the results to send on to the Reduce step. (Remember, the "no-op" Reducer will simply parrot every Map task's results.) The input key (the image file's name) is also the output key, in order to identify each image's results in the job's output.

While this job used a SequenceFile for input, it's just as easy to use a SequenceFile for output.

For example, consider a job that calls R to generate charts: you'd have to change the `Driver` class to specify SequenceFile output, and also change the Mapper's class definition and `map()` method to `Bytes Writable` (binary) output. Finally, you would have to use standard Java I/O to read the chart file into a `byte[]` array and put those bytes into the `BytesWritable`.

(Note that even though you'd be using a SequenceFile for input and output, your Mapper code only sees the `Text` and `BytesWritable` data types that are used inside the SequenceFile.)

Hadoop's Two Java APIs

Hadoop 0.20 is the current stable release, but some also say it's a transition state between 0.19 and 0.21. For this reason, Hadoop 0.20 contains both the old and new Java APIs.

The old API is technically deprecated as of 0.20, but the new API is still incomplete. I wrote the Java examples using the new API to future-proof the book. Hadoop 0.21 is already under active development, and the fact that the old API has been deprecated is a sign that the new API is the wave of the future.

Now let's look at the R script, `helper.R`, which is invoked by the Java code in Example 6-4:

```
dataFile <- commandArgs(trailingOnly=TRUE)  ❶
result <- imageFeatureExtraction( dataFile )  ❷
output.value <- paste( dataFile , result , sep="\t" )
```

❶ `commandArgs()` fetches the arguments passed to the R script, which in this case is the image's file name.

❷ Here, the mythical `imageFeatureExtraction()` function works on the provided file.

Running the Hadoop job: Let's say the Hadoop code is in a JAR named "launch-R.jar" and the input images are in a SequenceFile named `images-sample.seq`. Assuming the environment variables defined above, you can launch the job as follows:

```
${HADOOP_COMMAND} jar launch-R.jar \
    -files helper.R \ ❶
    /tmp/images-sample.seq \
    /tmp/hadoop-out
```

This command line is much shorter than the streaming command lines, mostly because several options are set in the driver class.

This is a typical Hadoop command line for Java jobs, with one exception:

❶ With a streaming job, your scripts magically appear on the cluster at runtime. When using the Java API, you have to use Hadoop's Distributed Cache (the `-files` flag) to copy `helper.R` to the cluster.

If you're testing the job on your workstation, in Hadoop's "local" (single-workstation) mode, you'll want to keep two ideas in mind:

For one, Distributed Cache doesn't really work in local mode. You'll want to launch the Hadoop command from the directory where `helper.R` lives such that the Mapper class can find it.

Secondly, the Hadoop job will treat the current directory as its runtime directory. That means the images extracted in the Mapper will be written to your current directory.

Reviewing the output: Let's assume the feature extraction function yields text output, so you would fetch and read it as explained in the previous examples. If your R code generates binary output, such as charts, you can write that as a SequenceFile: specify `SequenceFileOutputFormat` as the output, and have your Java code write the file's data to a `BytesWritable` object.

Caveats: This method keeps the entire job within Hadoop's walls: unlike the previous example, you're protected from machine crashes, network failures, and Hadoop's speculative execution. The cost is the extra overhead involved in putting all of your input data in SequenceFiles. Even if you're using `forqlift`, or you're comfortable writing a Hadoop Java job to do this, you still need to gather the inputs. That may involve a separate effort to copy the data from an existing service, such as an internal web server or file server.

Processing Related Groups (the Full Map and Reduce Phases)

Situation: You want to collect related records and operate on that group as a whole.

Returning to the "phone records" example, let's say you want to analyze every number's output call patterns. That would require you to first gather all of the calls made by each number (Map phase) and then process those records together (Reduce phase).

The code: As noted above, this will require both the Map and Reduce phases.

The Map phase code will extract the caller's phone number to use as the key, as shown in Example 6-4.

Example 6-4. mapper.R

```
#! /usr/bin/env Rscript

input <- file( "stdin" , "r" )
while( TRUE ){
    currentLine <- readLines( input , n=1 )
    if( 0 == length( currentLine ) ){
```

```
        break
    }

    currentFields <- unlist( strsplit( currentLine , "," ) )

    result <- paste(
        currentFields[1] ,
        currentLine ,
        sep="\t"
    )

    cat( result , "\n" )
}
close( input )
```

By now, the basic structure should look familiar. Remember that the first field in the comma-separated line is the caller's phone number, which serves as the key output from the Map task.

The Reducer code builds a `data.frame` of all calls made by each number, then passes the `data.frame` to the analysis function. Something to note here is that the logic in a Reducer script is different from that of a Map script. The flow may seem a little strange, so I'll explain it at a high level before showing the code sample.

In a Reducer script, each input line is of the format:

    {key}{tab}{value}

where {key} and {value} are a single key/value pair, as output from a Map task.

Recall that the Reducer's job is to collect all of the values for a given key, then process them together. Hadoop may pass a single Reducer values for multiple keys, but it will sort them first. When the key changes, then, you know you've seen all of the values for the previous key. You can process those values as a group, then move on to the next key.

With that in mind, a sample Reducer script for the call-analysis job is shown in Example 6-5.

Example 6-5. reducer.R

```
#! /usr/bin/env Rscript

input <- file( "stdin" , "r" )
lastKey <- ""

tempFile <- tempfile( pattern="hadoop-mr-demo-" , fileext="csv" ) ❶
tempHandle <- file( tempFile , "w" )

while( TRUE ){

    currentLine <- readLines( input , n=1 )
    if( 0 == length( currentLine ) ){
        break
    }
```

```
    tuple <- unlist( strsplit( currentLine , "\t" ) ) ❷
    currentKey <- tuple[1]
    currentValue <- tuple[2]

    if( ( currentKey != lastKey ) ){
        if( lastKey != "" ){  ❸
          close( tempHandle )
          bucket <- read.csv( tempFile , header=FALSE )  ❹
          result <- anotherCallAnalysisFunction( bucket )  ❺
          cat( currentKey , "\t" , result , "\n" )  ❻
          tempHandle <- file( tempFile , "w" )  ❼
        }

        lastKey <- currentKey  ❽
    }

    cat( currentLine , "\n" , file=tempHandle )  ❾
}

close( tempHandle )  ❿

bucket <- read.csv( tempFile , header=FALSE )
result <- anotherCallAnalysisFunction( bucket )
cat( currentKey , "\t" , result , "\n" )

unlink( tempFile )

close( input )
```

❶ Store the collected input lines in a temporary file. The input is in CSV form, so the code can call **read.csv()** on this temp file to build a **data.frame()**. (You could also build the **data.frame** in memory, one row at a time. The "right" way is whichever one works best for you.)

❷ Recall that a Map task outputs lines in **{key}{tab}{value}** form. Here, the code splits that line in order to address the key and value as separate variables.

❸ Check whether the key has changed. (The extra logic detects the initial condition of the key being blank.) The change in key is the cue to process the CSV data that has been accumulated into the temporary file from (1).

❹ Close off the temporary handle and read the file back in as a **data.frame** for easy processing.

❺ Pass that **data.frame** to the mythical **anotherCallAnalysisFunction()**, and collect its result.

❻ Write the result to standard output for Hadoop to collect. Make sure to include the key to tie these results to a particular phone number.

❼ Reopen the temp file for writing. This will zero it out, so it's ready for the next key's data.

❽ Update the key, such that the loop detects when the key changes again.

❾ Push a line to the temporary file for later processing.

❿ Repeat the end-of-key code, to process the data for the final key.

Running the Hadoop job:

```
${HADOOP_COMMAND} jar ${HADOOP_STREAMING_JAR} \
    \
    -D mapred.output.compress=true \
    -D mapred.output.compression.codec=${HADOOP_COMPRESSION_CODEC} \
    \
    -inputformat ${HADOOP_INPUTFORMAT} \
    -input /tmp/call-records.csv \
    -output /tmp/hadoop-out \
    -mappermapper.R \
    -reducer reducer.R
```

This is a standard Hadoop streaming command line. The only deviation from previous streaming command lines is that this one specifies a reducer script.

Reviewing the output: By now, you know how to explore both text and binary job output. This section is intentionally left blank.

Caveats: When you use the full Map and Reduce phases, you need to know how your data is distributed in terms of the keys output from the Map phase. This may require you to do some up-front exploratory data analysis before you can determine whether the job is truly Hadoop-worthy.

Generally speaking, the Map phase is very lightweight (since it's just used to assign keys to each input) and the heavy lifting takes place in the Reduce operation. To take advantage of the parallelism of the Reduce stage, then, you'll need to meet two conditions:

1. A large number of unique keys output from the Map phase
2. Each key should have a similar number of records (at least, no one key should clearly dominate)

Why is this? Say you have ten million input records. If the Map operation yields only two unique keys, each with five million records, then you will have two very long-running Reduce tasks and that would not be a scalable operation.

Alternatively, let's say the Map phase yields ten-thousand unique keys, but one of those keys has several million records. This would yield an unbalanced Reduce phase, in which the work for one key takes so long that it eliminates the gains from running the remaining keys' work in parallel.

I expect the phone records example is still a good fit for Hadoop parallelization since it is highly unlikely that one phone number made most of the calls. For your jobs, though, this may not be such a safe assumption.

This chapter covered a lot of ground, so let's take a step back to review when you'd want to use R+Hadoop and when you'd want to try another method.

When It Works...

Hadoop splits the work across a cluster, sending each unit of work to a different machine. Even though R itself is single-threaded, this simulates having one machine with tens or hundreds of CPUs at your disposal. Under ideal conditions—that you have the cluster to yourself for the evening—that means each execution of your R code gets all of a machine's RAM to itself. So you can say that R+Hadoop overcomes R's CPU and memory limitations.

...And When It Doesn't

Not completely spared from the memory wall: Hadoop is a *compute* solution, not a memory grid. If your job is so memory-intensive that a single task (Map or Reduce operation) outweighs the RAM on a single cluster node, Hadoop won't be of much use. In this case, you could try to decompose the job into even smaller pieces.

Needs infrastructure: R+Hadoop works best if you already have access to an in-house cluster. Elastic MapReduce, the cloud-based solution, runs a close second.

Building out a new cluster is no trivial matter. Businesses prefer that a new tool will pay for itself (in terms of increased profits, new revenue models, or reduced risk). Ask yourself whether your proposed Hadoop-based projects would outweigh the price tag for hardware, space, and maintenance.

Elastic MapReduce has its own pros and cons. From a business perspective, some people may be uncomfortable with their data leaving the office network to live in Amazon's cloud. (Regulatory compliance may also weigh heavily in this decision.) From a technical point of view, you have to consider the time required to ferry data to the cloud and back, as well as online storage costs.

Needs consistent cluster nodes: Hadoop executes your R scripts for you, and for streaming jobs it will even copy the R scripts to the cluster for you. It's otherwise up to you to keep the runtime environment consistent across the cluster. If your job requires a particular version of R, or specific R packages, your cluster admins will need to install those for you on *every cluster node* ahead of time.

This can be quite an adjustment for those who are accustomed to running their own, local copy of R on their workstation, where they can install any package they see fit. The solution here is social, not technical: avoid surprises. Make sure there is a clear path of communication between you and your cluster admins, and make sure you know what R packages are installed on the cluster *before* you prototype your job on your workstation. If you are your own cluster admin, you'll want to invest in tools such as Puppet, Chef, or cfengine to keep the machines consistent.

The Wrap-up

In this chapter, you learned a few ways to mix Hadoop and R. R+Hadoop gives you the most control and the most power, but comes at the cost of a Hadoop learning curve. In the next two chapters, you'll explore methods that abstract you from Hadoop, making them a little closer to "pure R" solutions.

## CHAPTER 7

RHIPE

This chapter is a guide to Saptarshi Guha's RHIPE package, the R and Hadoop Integrated Processing Environment. RHIPE's development history dates back to 2009 and it is still actively maintained by the original author.

Compared to R+Hadoop, RHIPE abstracts you from raw Hadoop but still requires an understanding of the MapReduce model.

Since you covered a lot of MapReduce and Hadoop details in the previous two chapters, this chapter will have a very short route to the examples.

Quick Look

Motivation: You like the power of MapReduce, as explained in the previous chapter, but you want something a little more R-centric.

Solution: Use the RHIPE R package as your Hadoop emissary. Even though you'll still have to understand MapReduce, you won't have to directly touch Hadoop.

Good because: You get Hadoop's power without leaving the comfy confines of R's language and interactive shell. (RHIPE even includes tools to work with HDFS.) This means you can MapReduce through a mountain of data during an interactive session of exploratory analysis.

How It Works

RHIPE sits between you and Hadoop. You write your Map and Reduce functions as R code, and RHIPE handles the scut work of invoking Hadoop commands.

To give you a quick example, here's a typical RHIPE call:

```
rhipe.job.def <- rhmr(
        map= ... block of R code for Mapper
        reduce= ... block of R code for Reducer
        ifolder="/path/to/input" ,
        ofolder="/path/to/output" ,
        ... a couple other RHIPE options
)

rhex( rhipe.job.ref )
```

That's it! There's no need to define separate scripts for the Map and Reduce stages, and you never run the hadoop command. I'll explain the details in the walkthrough section, but for now I just wanted to show you how easy RHIPE could be.

Setting Up

RHIPE is not yet hosted in CRAN, though the author expects that will soon change. For now, you can grab the source bundle from the project website at *http://ml.stat.purdue .edu/rhipe/*. Version 0.66 is current as of this writing. RHIPE releases are tied to specific versions of Hadoop and Google's ProtocolBuffers project, so pay close attention to the file you download to ensure compatibility.

Having downloaded the appropriate RHIPE version for your environment, installation is a snap:

```
export HADOOP_BIN=/path/to/bin/hadoop
R CMD INSTALL Rhipe_0.66.tar.gz
```

You'll need to install RHIPE on your local workstation as well as all cluster nodes. Be sure to note the path where RHIPE is installed on the cluster nodes: if it's not the same path as on your local workstation, you'll need add some extra statements to your code. I'll explain while walking you through the sample code.

 As of this writing, RHIPE is not compatible with Mac OS X Snow Leopard (10.6).

That's it for setup. You already understand MapReduce and Hadoop concepts, thanks to the previous two chapters, so you can dive right in to the examples.

Working with It

Phone Call Records, Redux

Situation: For a good compare/contrast exercise with R+Hadoop, this will repeat the first example from the previous chapter: you wish to analyze several million call records, each represented as a line of comma-separated text. This will be a Map-only job because you need just parallel execution but not any sort of grouping or sorting.

The code: Unlike R+Hadoop, everything you need is in a single R script, shown in Example 7-1.

Example 7-1. R script, first example

```
#! /usr/bin/env Rscript

library(Rhipe)

source.data.file <- "/tmp/call-data.csv.bz2"
output.folder <- "/tmp/rhipe-out"

map.block <- expression({ ❶


        map.function <- function( row ){
                currentFields <- unlist( strsplit( row , "," ) )

                result <- callAnalysis(
                        currentFields[1] , currentFields[2] , currentFields[3] ,
                        currentFields[4] , currentFields[5] , currentFields[6]
                )

                map.key <- currentFields[1]
                map.value <- result

                rhcollect( map.key , map.value ) ❷
                rhcounter( "map_task" , "handle_line" , 1 ) ❸
        }

        lapply( map.values , map.function )

})
config.block <- list( ❹
        mapred.map.tasks=200 , ❺
        mapred.reduce.tasks=0 ,
        mapred.task.timeout=600000 ,
        mapred.output.compress="true" ,
        mapred.output.compression.codec="org.apache.hadoop.io.compress.BZip2Codec"
)
```

```
options.block <- rhoptions() ❻
options.block$runner[1] <- "/usr/local/lib/R/site-library/Rhipe/libs/imperious.so"

## ... continued in next code listing
```

Some of the code was lifted from a previous example, so I'll focus on what's new this time around:

❶ `map.block` is the R code that will be run for each Map task. Similar to the Map scripts used in Hadoop streaming, a RHIPE Map task expects to receive multiple input lines. (This differs from Hadoop's Java API, in which the Map operation receives a single input record.) A few lines down, the code uses `lapply()` to invoke `map.function()` on each line of input.

❷ In R+Hadoop, a Map block emits a key/value pair to standard output. In a RHIPE job, call `rhcollect()` to emit a key/value pair from Map task.

❸ Hadoop counters serve a dual purpose. For one, they are useful for keeping track of task execution. Two, they serve as a beacon of activity such that the cluster knows a job is still running. (Recall, Hadoop will kill a job it determines to be inactive for too long.) Here the `rhcounter()` command increments a custom counter that tracks the number of times the Mapper successfully processes a line of input. You'll see several other counters throughout these examples. A little later, I'll show you how to fetch these counters' values.

❹ Even though RHIPE abstracts you from Hadoop, you can still set Hadoop options using a standard `list`. (A little later in the code, another RHIPE command will accept this list.) You've already seen the properties to disable the reduce phase, compress the output, and set the task timeout. I'll discuss the new property next.

❺ R+Hadoop uses `NLineInputFormat` to split a job's input, one line per Map task, such that the job is balanced across the cluster. In RHIPE you explicitly set the number of map tasks using the Hadoop configuration property `mapred.map.tasks`. (Here, the number 200 was a best guess based on the size of my sample input compared to the strength of my test cluster. In turn, you'll need to have similar information to set this value for your own jobs.)

❻ It's entirely possible that RHIPE is not installed to the same place on your cluster nodes as on your local workstation. For example, you may have R packages in a personal area under `/home`, whereas the cluster nodes use a system-wide path under `/usr`. To let RHIPE know this, you modify the field `runner` in the job's configuration options. The path may be different on your cluster. Ask your cluster admins if you are not sure.

The R commands to build and launch a RHIPE job are included in Example 7-2. They bear a striking resemblance to the sample RHIPE call I shared in the beginning of this chapter.

Example 7-2. R script, continued

```
rhinit(TRUE,TRUE,buglevel=2000) ❶

rhipe.job.def <- rhmr( ❷
        jobname="RHIPE example 1" ,

        map=map.block ,

        mapred=config.block ,

        opts=options.block ,

        ifolder=source.data.file ,
        ofolder=output.folder ,

        inout=c( "text" , "text" ) ❸

)

rhipe.job.result <- rhex( rhipe.job.def ) ❹
```

❶ You must initialize RHIPE once in your R session before you prepare a job. RHIPE will provide extra output if you pass the values TRUE,TRUE,buglevel=2000 to rhinit. I encourage you to do this, especially during your early RHIPE experiments, because it's so helpful for debugging.

❷ The command rhmr() builds a job. It accepts all of the objects defined earlier: map is the block of code for the Mapper; mapred is the list of Hadoop configuration properties; and opts is the RHIPE configuration object. (You could also define those objects in-line as you pass them to rhmr() but that would make for messy code.) The parameter ifolder can refer to a single HDFS input file or an HDFS directory that contains several files. ofolder specifies the directory, also in HDFS, to store the job's output.

❸ Values of the inout vector indicate the format RHIPE will use for the job's input and output, respectively. text is the line-by-line plaintext format we all know and love. lapply is helpful for certain parameter sweeps: pass N=value to rhmr() and RHIPE will feed your Map task the numbers 1 through value as input. (In this case, you would omit rhmr()'s ifolder parameter.) sequence uses Hadoop SequenceFiles, but with special RHIPE data types. Check out the sidebar, "Can RHIPE Handle SequenceFiles? Yes...and No" on page 90 for details.

❹ Call rhex() to launch your job on the Hadoop cluster.

Can RHIPE Handle SequenceFiles? Yes…and No

I described Hadoop SequenceFiles archive in Chapter 5, and I provided an example of how to use them in Chapter 6. Those SequenceFiles used standard Hadoop data types, `Text` and `BytesWritable`, to store text and raw binary information, respectively.

RHIPE can use SequenceFiles as storage for native R objects, such as `list` and `data.frame`. The catch? RHIPE uses a custom data type called `RHBytesWritable` to store that data. As of this writing, `RHIPE` only understands SequenceFiles it has created. This means you cannot, say, pack a SequenceFile full of images and process them through `RHIPE`.

This may limit a `RHIPE` SequenceFile's potential as a general storage mechanism, but it's still useful as a cache or intermediate storage option between `RHIPE` jobs. For example, you could define one job that converts raw data into a `RHIPE`-format Sequence-File, and other `RHIPE` jobs could use that file as input for further processing.

Running the Hadoop job: Running a `RHIPE` job is a one-liner, and it's familiar to a great many users of R:

```
export HADOOP_BIN=/path/to/bin/hadoop
R --vanilla --file=example1.R
```

You could also run these statements from R's shell or your preferred IDE. (In the latter case, be sure to define the `HADOOP_BIN` environment variable before you launch the IDE.)

RHIPE will translate your R statements into Hadoop-speak, run the job, and return control to your terminal so you can execute more statements.[*] In the next example I'll show you how to read the job's output back into your R session for further manipulation.

Reviewing the output: At the start of this example, I mentioned how to use `rhcounter()` to increment custom counters. When your job completes, `rhex()` returns and you can print the result object to see the job's counters. You'll see the custom counters defined in the your code, as well as some built-in values.

Inspecting these counters is a good way to spot-check the job's results. For example: "do we see the expected number of input and output records for each phase?" In the sample output below, note the `map_block` group and its `enter` counter: this is defined in the `map.block` code, and increments every time RHIPE enters the block of Mapper code. If this number is smaller than expected, there may be some number of problematic input records (such as malformed lines).

(I've slightly reordered the output for clarity, shown in Example 7-3.)

---

[*] In this way, using RHIPE is a little like using Pig, the Hadoop data-flow language with an interactive shell. You can visit the Pig website at *http://pig.apache.org/* for details.

Example 7-3. Counter values from a small test-run

```
> rhipe.job.result$counters
$map_task
success
   2689
```

```
$`Map-Reduce Framework`
        Combine input records        Combine output records
                        0                            0
          Map input records            Map output bytes
                     2689                        62574

Map output materialized bytes         Map output records
                     9410                         2689

           Reduce input groups         Reduce input records
                     1083                         2689

         Reduce output records         Reduce shuffle bytes
                     1083                            0
            Spilled Records             SPLIT_RAW_BYTES
                     5378                          149
```

```
$`File Input Format Counters `
Bytes Read
     588053
```

```
$`File Output Format Counters `
Bytes Written
        15826
```

That's a look into the job's result status. The job's *output data* is sitting in a text file in HDFS. You can use standard Hadoop shell commands to display it on your terminal (`hadoop fs -cat`) or copy it back to your workstation (`hadoop fs -get`). You can also use RHIPE commands to pull data straight from HDFS into your R session. I'll explain how to do that in the next example. Finally, you can leave the output data in HDFS to serve as input data for another job. This way, you could use RHIPE to create a workflow of chained Hadoop jobs for multiple stages of analysis or transformation.

Tweet Brevity

This demonstrates a RHIPE job that uses the full Map and Reduce phases.

Situation: You've collected some large number of tweets, and you want to calculate each author's average number of characters per tweet. ("Is anyone particularly brief?" "Who brushes against that 140-character limit?") This sounds pleasantly amenable to MapReduce: group the tweets by the author's name, then analyze the contents of each group.

Example 7-4. Tweet brevity example

```
#! /usr/bin/env Rscript

library(Rhipe)

source.data.file <- "/tmp/small-sample-tweets.dat.bz2"
output.folder <- "/tmp/rhipe-out"

setup.block <- list( ❶
        map=expression({
                home.Rlib <- "/path/to/your/local/R/libraries"
                invisible( .libPaths( c( home.Rlib , .libPaths() ) ) )
                library(RJSONIO)
        }) ,
        reduce=expression({ })
)

config.block <- list(
        mapred.output.compress="true" ,
        mapred.output.compression.codec="org.apache.hadoop.io.compress.BZip2Codec" ,
        mapred.task.timeout=600000
)

map.block <- expression({

        rhcounter( "map_stage" , "enter_block" , 1 )

        map.function <- function( tweet.raw ){
                tryCatch({
                        tweet <- fromJSON( tweet.raw ) ❷
                        chars.in.tweet <- nchar( tweet$text )
                        rhcollect( tweet$user$screen_name , chars.in.tweet )
                        rhcounter( "map_stage" , "success" , 1 )
                } ,
                error=function( error ){
                        rhcounter( "map_stage" , "error" , 1 )
                        print( error )
                })
        }

        lapply( map.values , map.function )
})

## continues ...
```

❶ setup.block defines code that RHIPE will execute on each node before launching the Map and Reduce phases. If you require packages that aren't in the system R library paths, you'll have to manually update the paths as shown in the call to .lib Paths(). Tweet streams are typically JSON data, so the Mapper setup expression loads the RJSONIO package[†] to parse the input.

[†] By Duncan Temple Lang, *http://cran.r-project.org/web/packages/RJSONIO/index.html*

❷ RJSONIO's `fromJSON()` parses the tweet into a simple R object. The author's Twitter screen name serves as the output key, and the tweet's length as the output value.

Example 7-5. Tweet brevity example, continued (part 2)

```
reduce.block <- expression(
     pre = { ❶
               tweetCount <- 0
               tweetLength <- 0
               currentKey <- reduce.key
               rhcounter( "reduce_stage" , "pre" , 1 )
     } ,
     reduce = { ❷
               tweetCount <- tweetCount + length( reduce.values )
               tweetLength <- tweetLength + sum( unlist( reduce.values ) )
               rhcounter( "reduce_stage" , "reduce" , 1 )
     } ,
     post = { ❸
               mean.length <- as.integer( round(tweetLength/tweetCount) )
               rhcollect( currentKey , mean.length )
               rhcounter( "reduce_stage" , "post" , 1 )
     }
)
## continues ...
```

A RHIPE Reducer is more straightforward than its Hadoop streaming equivalent, but it still requires a little explanation. It's comprised of three code blocks: `pre`, `reduce`, and `post`.

❶ The `pre` block is executed once per key. You can use this space to define variables that will be used in the `reduce` and `post` blocks. This example defines variables to track the total number and length of tweets from this author. (Compared to Hadoop streaming, notice that your RHIPE Reducer code doesn't have to keep track of the keys.)

❷ RHIPE hands the `reduce` block some values for the current key. Those appear as a list called `reduce.values`. You can use the `reduce` block to aggregate any data across all of the values for a given key. Here, the code uses the data in `reduce.values` to update the tweet count and length.

❸ By the time RHIPE executes the `post` block, it has processed all of the values for the current key. This is the place to wrap up any calculations based on the values you updated or collected in the `reduce` block. In this example, the `post` block calculates the mean tweet length based on this author's total count and number of tweets.

You may see some RHIPE code in the wild that omits the `pre` and `post` blocks of the Reducer, and does everything in the `reduce` block. In turn, you may wonder: *Why does that code work? I thought RHIPE only passed my Reducer a few values at a time?*

By default, RHIPE passes the reduce block *a lot* of values. The default is so large—10,000 values—that it may exceed the number of values for a given key, in which case you can get away with using just a reduce block in your Reducer.

Just because it works doesn't mean it's good form. You want to develop the habit of using pre, reduce, and post blocks in your RHIPE-related code. It may seem wasteful, but it will spare you the future headache of debugging strange Reducer behavior: "It works in my local dev environment (on a small sample), but not in production..." or the slightly more insidious, "It works for some keys, but not others."

Example 7-6. Tweet brevity example, continued (part 3)

```
rhinit(TRUE,TRUE,buglevel=2000)

options.block <- rhoptions()
options.block$runner[1] <- "/usr/local/lib/R/site-library/Rhipe/libs/imperious.so"

rhipe.job.def <- rhmr( ❶
        jobname="rhipe example 2" ,

        setup=setup.block ,
        map=map.block ,
        reduce=reduce.block ,

        opts=options.block ,

        mapred=config.block ,

        ifolder=source.data.file ,
        ofolder=output.folder ,
        inout=c( "text" , "text" )
)

rhipe.job.result <- rhex( rhipe.job.def )
## continues ...
```

❶ Remember to pass the reduce block and the setup block to rhmr().

Running the Hadoop job: As described in the previous example, you can run this as an R script from the command line or as statements in R's console.

Reviewing the output: Once rhex() completes, it returns control to your R terminal. The job's result data sits in HDFS right now, but you can then read that back into your R session for further manipulation. Let's see how that works in Example 7-7.

Example 7-7. Tweet brevity example, continued (part 4)

```
output.data <- rhread( paste( output.folder , "/part-*" , sep="" ) , type="text" ) ❶

library(plyr) ❷

tweet.means <- mdply(
        output.data ,
        function( line ){
```

```
            line <- gsub( "\r$" , "" , output.data ) ❸
            tuple <- unlist( strsplit( line , "\t" ) )

            return( data.frame( tname=tuple[1] , tcount=as.integer(tuple[2]) ))
        },
        .expand=FALSE
)
```

❶ Invoke rhread() to pull HDFS data into R. Here, rhread() accepts the path to the job's output directory and a glob expression that will pick up all of the data files. (The output directory may also contain other files, such as a _SUCCESS if the job finished without error.) If you specify type=text, rhread() will return a one-column Matrix of string values, one row for each line of output. For SequenceFiles, specify type=sequence and rhread() will return a list of values.

❷ Hadley Wickham's plyr package‡ will make it easy to transform the matrix provided by rhread().

❸ plyr's mdply() accepts a matrix and applies the supplied function to each row. Rows of the matrix output.data are of the format {key}{tab}{value}{carriage return} so the call to gsub() removes the trailing carriage return and then splits the line by the tab character. The inline function returns a one-row data.frame, with columns for the tweet author's name (tname) and average tweet length (value). mdply() combines all of those function calls' results into a single data.frame that is assigned to tweet.means.

Having imported the Hadoop job's data back into an R-friendly format, you can perform further processing as part of an interactive data analysis session.

rhread() is one of several HDFS commands provided by RHIPE. Please see the sidebar "Other Useful RHIPE Commands" for the rest.

Other Useful RHIPE Commands

RHIPE isn't just an abstraction for running Hadoop MapReduce jobs. It also includes some commands to work with HDFS:

rhread() *and* rhwrite()
    Read from and write to data stored in HDFS.

rhget() *and* rhput()
    Copy HDFS files to and from your local filesystem.

rhls()
    List files in HDFS.

rhdel()
    Remove files in HDFS.

---

‡ If you haven't used plyr before, you'll want to give it a try. Think of it as sapply() or lapply(), but less arcane. *http://plyr.had.co.nz/*

More Complex Tweet Analysis

Situation: You need to pass complex data types between Map and Reduce stages; simple strings and numeric types will not suffice.

The code: In the previous example, you needed to pass just the author's name and tweet length from the Mappers to the Reducers. That was easy: the code just passed the name (a string) and length (a number) to `rhcollect()` as output key and output value, respectively.

A tweet is a rich data object, though, so it's not unlikely that you'd want extract even more information. Let's say that, this time around, you've written a custom analysis function that wants a `data.frame` of the tweet text, user mentions within the tweet, number of retweets, and so on.

One option would be to call `paste()` to concatenate those values into a delimited string in the Map phase, then call `strsplit()` to unpack that string in the Reduce phase. (This is, in effect, what you have to do for R+Hadoop.)

You could still do that with `RHIPE`, but there's no reason. Remember when I said that `RHIPE` can read and write special SequenceFiles that hold native R objects? It also uses those to transfer data between the Map and Reduce phases. In the Map task, then, you can pass a `data.frame`, a `list`, or pretty much any other native R object to `rhcollect()`. You'll get the same object back in a Reduce task without any translation effort on your part.[§] This is one key strength of `RHIPE` over R+Hadoop: you're talking native R the whole time.

Example 7-8 demonstrates those ideas in code.

Example 7-8. Passing complex values

```
## setup.block and config.list are the same as in the previous example,
## so we omit them here
map.block <- expression({

        rhcounter( "map_stage" , "enter_block" , 1 )

        map.function <- function( tweet.raw ){
                tryCatch({
                        tweet <- fromJSON( tweet.raw )

                        reply_user_id <- ifelse( is.null( tweet$in_reply_to_user_id ) ,
                            NA , tweet$in_reply_to_user_id )
                        geo <- ifelse( is.null( tweet$geo ) ,  NA , tweet$geo )
                        mentions <- ifelse( is.null( tweet$user_mentions ) , 0 ,
                            length( is.null( tweet$user_mentions ) ) ) )
```

[§] For the sticklers, it won't be the same "object" in the sense of "location in memory"; it will be an *equivalent* object that contains the same fields with the same values.

```
                    tuple <- data.frame( ❶
                            screen_name=tweet$user$screen_name ,
                            in_reply_to=reply_user_id ,
                            create_time=tweet$created_at ,
                            retweet_count=tweet$retweet_count ,
                            user_mentions=mentions ,
                            location=geo ,
                            text=tweet$text
                    )

                    rhcollect( tweet$user$screen_name , tuple ) ❷
                    rhcounter( "map_stage" , "success" , 1 )
            } ,
            error=function( error ){
                    rhcounter( "map_stage" , "error" , 1 )
                    print( error )
            })
        }

        lapply( map.values , map.function )
})

## continues ...
```

❶ Collect the extracted data into a `data.frame`.

❷ Pass that `data.frame` to `rhcollect()`, just the same as you've been passing simple strings and numbers. No fuss, no muss, nothing special to do here.

Example 7-9. Passing complex values, continued (part 2)

```
reduce.block <- expression(
        pre = {
                df <- data.frame() ❶
                currentKey <- reduce.key
                rhcounter( "reduce_stage" , "pre" , 1 )
        } ,
        reduce = {
                df.tmp <- do.call( rbind , reduce.values ) ❷
                df <- rbind( df , df.tmp )
                rhcounter( "reduce_stage" , "reduce" , 1 )
        } ,
        post = {
                result <- tweetAnalysis( df ) ❸
                rhcollect( currentKey , result )
                rhcounter( "reduce_stage" , "post" , 1 )
        }
)

rhinit(TRUE,TRUE,buglevel=2000)
## continues ...
```

❶ Start with a single, empty `data.frame`. Code in the `reduce` block will add rows.

❷ The call to `rbind()` will append this run's values to the `data.frame` defined in the pre block.

❸ The custom `tweetAnalysis()` function accepts the `data.frame`, fully populated with all of this author's tweet data.frame+ to

Example 7-10. Passing complex values, continued (part 3)

```
rhipe.job.def <- rhmr(
        jobname="rhipe tweet test" ,

        setup=setup.block ,
        map=map.block ,
        reduce=reduce.block ,

        opts=options.block ,

        mapred=config.block ,

        ifolder=source.data.file ,
        ofolder=output.folder ,
        inout=c( "text" , "text" ) ❶
)

rhipe.job.result <- rhex( rhipe.job.def )
```

❶ Note that the job uses use text data for input and output, even though RHIPE used a SequenceFile behind the scenes to transfer our `data.frame` between the Mappers and Reducers.

 Remember earlier, when I mentioned that you could save native R objects to a RHIPE SequenceFile? All you have to do is pass those objects to `rhcollect()` in the Reducer. Make sure you set the second value of `inout` to sequence. That's it.

Running the Hadoop job: You know what to do here...

Reviewing the output: The job's output would be a typical set of tab-delimited key/value lines, with the output of our mythical `tweetAnalysis()` function as the value. You could call `rhread()` to pull it back into your R session, or one of `rhget()` or `hadoop fs -get` to bring it back to your local workstation.

When It Works...

RHIPE lets you run Hadoop jobs without leaving R. That's not just a useful abstraction, it's also a powerful concept: it means you can apply MapReduce to large-scale datasets while performing interactive, exploratory data analysis. It's like having massive cluster compute power at your fingertips. (Exploratory analysis with R+Hadoop is not impossible, but more cumbersome, and certainly not of the "interactive" variety.)

This is also more in-tune with an R workflow: I typically see people use Hadoop to boil a dataset down to a more manageable size, then load those results back into R for charting and such. RHIPE lets you skip the middle step because you never leave R.

 If most of your RHIPE time involves basic data sorting, filtering, or transformation work, and doesn't require special R packages, you may want to look into Pig. Like R, Pig is a scripting language with an interactive shell. Like RHIPE, Pig transforms your statements into Hadoop code on the fly. Unlike R, Pig was built for Hadoop from the very start, and you can install it without touching your Hadoop cluster. For more details, please check out the Pig website at *http://pig.apache.org* and *Programming Pig* by Alan F. Gates (O'Reilly).

...And When It Doesn't

Installation woes: You'll need to install RHIPE on every cluster node, which means you'll need to make a small sacrifice to your cluster admins.

Those of you running a cloud-based cluster will have extra legwork to do. Building RHIPE requires a specific version of Google's Protocol Buffers. If your chosen image doesn't provide that precompiled,‖ you'll have to build it yourself.

Finally, if you're using an ephemeral cluster (such as those created by Elastic MapReduce or Whirr) you'll have to package up the install routine into something scriptable.# While this hardly a show-stopper, I feel it's worthy of mention because such cluster maintenance duties distract you from your main purpose of data analysis.

RHIPE's author, Saptarshi Guha, says the next version will be designed for Hadoop 0.21 and incompatible with 0.20. This is especially of interest to those in a hosted Hadoop environment, such as Elastic MapReduce, where you are bound to a particular version of Hadoop.

Finally, as of this writing, RHIPE is not compatible with Mac OS X Snow Leopard (10.6).

Documentation: RHIPE has plenty of documentation, available online as HTML and offline as a PDF. That said, there's no help in R format, so you can't type "`help( rhinit )`" or "`?rhex`" to get help while in the R shell. That also confounds R-enabled editors and IDEs that show you a function's help as you type its name.

This will be less of a problem as you grow accustomed to using RHIPE; but it can steepen the learning curve of your early experiments.

‖ For example, many Debian 5 and Ubuntu 10 AMIs ship with an older version of Protocol Buffers

#For example, I keep a copy of the RHIPE source code on a public S3 bucket. That reduces download time and insulates me from any connectivity issues to RHIPE's hosting.

No support for generic SequenceFiles: RHIPE can only understand SequenceFiles it has created, which means it cannot (directly) work with binary input or output data. If you're looking to process binary data, you could try the workarounds described in Example 6-2 in Chapter 6.

The Wrap-up

You've just experienced a tour of RHIPE, which gives you Hadoop power from R's command shell. Don't be fooled by the list of caveats above: RHIPE is very powerful and fits into a lot of situations where those drawbacks are insignificant or even non-issues.

Now that you've seen R+Hadoop and RHIPE, it's time for the book's third and final Hadoop-related R project: Segue.

## CHAPTER 8

Segue

Welcome to the last of the book's recipes for R parallelism. This will be a short chapter, but don't let that fool you: Segue's scope is intentionally narrow. This focus makes it a particularly powerful tool.

Segue's mission is as simple as it gets: make it easy to use Elastic MapReduce as a parallel backend for `lapply()`-style operations. So easy, in fact, that it boasts of doing this in only two lines of R code.[*]

This narrow focus is no accident. Segue's creator, JD Long, wanted occasional access to a Hadoop cluster to run his pleasantly parallel,[†] computationally expensive models. Elastic MapReduce was a great fit but still a bit cumbersome for his workflow. He created Segue to tackle the grunt work so he could focus on his higher-level modeling tasks.

Segue is a relatively young package. Nonetheless, since its creation in 2010, it has attracted a fair amount of attention.

Quick Look

Motivation: You want Hadoop power to drive some `lapply()` loops, perhaps for a parameter sweep, but you want minimal Hadoop contact. You consider MapReduce to be too much of a distraction from your work.

Solution: Use the `segue` package's `emrlapply()` to send your calculations up to Elastic MapReduce, the Amazon Web Services cloud-based Hadoop product.

Good because: You get to focus on your modelling work, while `segue` takes care of transforming your `lapply()` work into a Hadoop job.

---

[*] Segue's original slogan was a bit spicier, which is a nice way of saying that it's not printable. JD has since softened the message, but it's hard not to appreciate the original slogan's enthusiasm.

[†] Sometimes known as "embarrassingly parallel," though we can't fathom what could possibly be embarassing about parallel computation.

How It Works

Segue takes care of launching the Elastic MapReduce cluster, shipping data back and forth, and all other such housekeeping. As such, it abstracts you from having to know much about Hadoop, and even Elastic MapReduce. Your monthly bill from Amazon Web Services will be your only real indication that you've done anything beyond standard R.

Still, there is a catch: I emphasize that Segue is designed for CPU-intensive jobs across a large number of inputs, such as parameter sweeps. If you have data-intensive work, or only a few inputs, Segue will not shine. Also, Segue works *only* with Elastic Map-Reduce. It cannot talk to your in-house Hadoop cluster.

Setting Up

Segue requires that you have an AWS account. (Be sure to enable the Elastic MapReduce service.) If you haven't already done this, you'll want to grab your preferred credit card and head over to *http://aws.amazon.com/*.

I'd also suggest you run one of Amazon's sample Elastic MapReduce jobs so you can familiarize yourself with the AWS console. It will come in handy later, when you double-check that your cluster has indeed shutdown. I'll discuss that part shortly. For the remainder of this chapter, though, I'll assume you're familiar with AWS concepts.

Next, install Segue. It isn't available on CRAN, so grab the source bundle from the project website at *http://code.google.com/p/segue/* and run:

```
R CMD INSTALL {file}
```

from your OS command line.

 As of this writing, Segue does not run under Windows.

Working with It

Model Testing: Parameter Sweep

Segue has only one use case, so I have just one example to show you.

Situation: You're doing a parameter sweep across a large number of inputs, and running it locally using `lapply()` just takes too long.

The code: To set the stage, let's say you have a function `runModel()` that takes a single list as input. You wrap up the entire set of inputs in a parent list (that is, a list-of-lists) called `input.list`. To execute `runModel()` on each sub-list, you could use the standard `lapply()` like so:

```
runModel <- function( params ){ ... }
input.list <- list( ... each element is also a list ... )

lapply.result <- lapply( input.list , runModel )
```

So far, this is nothing new, and it works fine for most cases. If `input.list` contains enough elements and each iteration of `runModel()` takes a few minutes, though, this exercise could run for several hours on your local workstation. We'll show you how to transform that `lapply()` call into the Segue equivalent.

Segue setup:

```
library(segue)

setCredentials( "your AWS access key", "your AWS secret key" ) ❶

emr.handle <- createCluster( ❷
        numInstances=6 ,
        ec2KeyName="...your AWS SSH key..."
)
```

This first R excerpt prepares your environment by loading the Segue library and launching your cluster. Of note:

❶ The call to `setCredentials()` accepts your AWS credentials. Understandably, not everyone wants to embed passwords in a script or type them into the R console (where they'll end up in your `.Rhistory` file). As an alternative, Segue can pull those values from the environment variables `AWSACCESSKEY` and `AWSSECRETKEY`. Be sure to define these variables *before* you launch R.

❷ `createCluster()` connects to Amazon and builds your cluster. The `numInstances` parameter specifies the number of nodes (machine instances) in the cluster. A value of `1` means all the work will take place on a single node, a combined master and worker. For some larger value *N*, there will always be *N-1* worker nodes and one master node. In other words, there's not much difference between `numInstances=1` and `numInstances=2` since you'll have just a single worker node in either case.

Why, then, would a person want `numInstances=1`? You could use this for testing, or for those cases in which you just want a separate machine to do the heavy lifting. Consider your local machine is a netbook or some other resource-constrained hardware. You could use Segue to offload the big calculations to a single-node cluster, then use your local machine for simple plots and smaller calculations.

Recall that Hadoop splits up your input to distribute work throughout the cluster. Segue's author recommends at least ten input items for each worker node. A smaller input list may lead to an imbalance, with one node taking on most of the work.

`createCluster()` will print log messages while the launch and bootstrap take place, and return control to your R console once the cluster is ready for action. Its return value `emr.handle` is a handle to the remote EMR cluster. Save this, as you'll need it to send work to the cluster, and also to shut it down later.

Now, you're ready to run the `lapply()` loop on the cluster, Segue-style:

```
emr.result <- emrlapply(emr.handle , input.list , runModel, taskTimeout=10 )
```

`emrlappy()` looks and acts very much like an `lapply()` call, doesn't it? The only new parameters are the cluster handle `emr.handle` and the task timeout `taskTimeout`. (I discussed Hadoop task timeouts in Chapter 6.) Here, the timeout is set to ten minutes.

Behind the scenes, Segue has packed up your data, shipped it to the cloud, run the job, collected the output data, and brought it back to you safe and sound. As far as you can see from your R console, though, nothing out of the ordinary has happened. Such is the beauty of Segue.

Reviewing the output: There's surprisingly little to explain as far as reviewing output from `emrlapply()`: if you feed `lapply()` and `emrlapply()` the same input, they should return the same values. That means `emrlapply()` is an almost seamless replacement for `lapply()` in your typical R workflow (at least for `lapply()` calls that have suitably sized inputs). We emphasize "almost" seamless, because there is one catch: `emrlapply()` expects a plain `list` as input, whereas `lapply()` will attempt to munge a non-`list` to a `list`.

 Because `lapply()` and `emrlapply()` are so similar, you can test your code on a small sample set using the former, before launching a cluster to run the latter.

Speaking of workflows, I'd like to emphasize that you can use the same cluster handle for many calls to `emrlapply()`. You don't have to launch a new cluster for each `emrl apply()` call. For example, you could use Segue to launch a cluster in the morning, call `emrlapply()` several times during the day, and then shut down the cluster in the evening. This is very important to know, since that initial call to `createCluster()` can take several minutes to return. You probably don't want to do that several times a day.

Eventually, though, you'll run out of work to do, at which point you'll want to shut-down your EMR cluster. Simply call Segue's `stopCluster()`:

```
stopCluster(emr.handle)
```

Keep in mind that there are only two ways to terminate the cluster:

- Call `stopCluster()` from your R console
- Use AWS tools (such as the AWS web console, or the command-line Elastic Map-Reduce toolset) to terminate the EMR job

Did you notice something missing? *"Quit R" is not on this list, because closing R will not terminate the cluster.*

To spare you an unexpectedly large AWS bill, I'll even put this inside a warning box for you:

 The cluster will keep running until you actively shut it down by terminating the EMR job. Even if you close R, or your local workstation crashes, your EMR cluster will keep running and Amazon will continue to bill you for the time.

This is one reason to you familiarize yourself with the Elastic MapReduce tab of the AWS console: should your local workstation crash, or you otherwise lose the cluster handle returned by `startCluster()`, you'll have to manually terminate the cluster.

When It Works...

Segue very much abstracts you from Hadoop, Elastic MapReduce, and even Amazon Web Services. As such, it is the "most R" (or, if you prefer, "least Hadoop") of the Hadoop-related strategies presented in this book. If your goal is to run a large `lapply()`-style calculation and get on with the rest of your R work, Segue wins hands-down compared to R+Hadoop and `RHIPE`.

...And When It Doesn't

Tied to Amazon's cloud: Segue only works with Elastic MapReduce. This means it won't help you take advantage of your in-house Hadoop cluster, or your self-managed cluster in the cloud.

(This is part of why Segue isn't helpful for data-intensive work: data transformation and transfer to and from Amazon's cloud would counteract the benefits of making your `lapply()` loop run in parallel.)

Requires extra responsibility: By default, Elastic MapReduce builds an ephemeral cluster that lasts only as long as a job's runtime. Segue, on the other hand, tells EMR to leave the cluster running after the first job completes. That leaves it to you to check and double-check that you've truly terminated the cluster when you're done running jobs.

Granted, this is a concern when you use *any* cloud resources. I mention it here because Segue shields you so well from the cluster build-out that it's easy to forget you've left anything running. Beware, then, and make a habit to regularly check your AWS account's billing page.‡

Limited scope: Segue has just one use case, and that narrow focus is its blessing as well as its curse. If all you want is to turbo-charge your `lapply()` loops with little distraction from your everyday R work, Segue is a great fit. If you need anything else, or if you live to twiddle Hadoop clusters by hand, Segue will not make you very happy.

The Wrap-up

Segue is designed to do one thing, and do it well: use Amazon's Elastic MapReduce as a backend for `lapply()`-style work. It abstracts you from Hadoop and other technical details, which makes it useful for people who find cluster management a real distraction from their R work.

---

‡ I was once bitten by cluster resources gone awry (not related to Segue) and have since made a habit of checking the AWS Billing page on a regular basis. Amazon, if you're listening: could you please provide an API to check billing? Thank you.

## CHAPTER 9

New and Upcoming

A perfect world would let us stop time to research and write, since a technical book covers a moving target. We didn't have such a luxury, so instead we set aside some space to pick up on some new arrivals.

This chapter mentions a few tools for which we could have provided more coverage, had we been willing to postpone the book's release date. Think of this as a look into one possible future of R parallelism. Special thanks to our colleagues, reviewers, and friends who so kindly brought these to our attention.

doRedis

The foreach() function[*] executes an arbitrary R expression across an input. foreach()'s strength is that it can execute *in parallel* with the help of a supplied parallel backend. The doRedis package provides such a backend, using the Redis datastore[†] as a job queue.

doRedis can work locally to take advantage of multicore systems, and also farm tasks out to remote R instances ("workers"). It's straightforward to add or remove workers at runtime—even in mid-job—to adapt to changing work conditions or speed up job processing. Similar to Hadoop, doRedis is fault-tolerant in that failed tasks are automatically resubmitted to their job queue.

doRedis supports Linux, Mac OS X, and Windows systems.

- Description: *http://bigcomputing.com/doRedis.html*
- Source: *http://github.com/bwlewis/doRedis*

---

[*] *http://cran.r-project.org/web/packages/foreach/*

[†] *http://redis.io/*

RevoScale R and RevoConnectR (RHadoop)

Revolution Analytics is a company that provides R tools, support, and training. They have two products of note.

First up is the commercial Revolution R Enterprise. The current beta release includes *RevoScaleR* (RSR), which brings distributed computing to R. When you use the special *XDF* data format, RSR functions know to work on that data one chunk at a time, which addresses R's memory limitations. (This is not unlike Hadoop+HDFS.) To address R's CPU limitations, RSR includes functions to run code across several local cores, or across a cluster of machines running using MS Windows HPC Server.‡

Second, and more recently, the Revolution gang released the open-source *RHadoop* packages (also known as *RevoConnectR*) to marry Hadoop and R: `rmr` provides the core MapReduce functionality; `rhdfs` routines let you manage data in HDFS; and `rhbase` talks to HBase, the Hadoop-backed database. We're especially interested in `rmr`, which strives to be a clean, intuitive way to access Hadoop power without leaving the R comfort zone. RHadoop is still young, but we think it has strong potential.

Both RSR and `rmr` fold into your typical data analysis work: you use special functions and constructs to get the essence of a larger dataset, then pass those results to standard R functions for plotting and further analysis.

- Revolution R Enterprise and RevoScaleR: *http://www.revolutionanalytics.com/*
- RHadoop: *https://github.com/RevolutionAnalytics/RHadoop/wiki*

cloudNumbers.com

cloudnumbers.com is a platform for on-demand distributed, parallel computing. It provides out-of-the-box support for R as well as C/C++ and Python. We see cloudnumbers.com as a cousin of Amazon's EC2, but specialized for scientific HPC work.

That said, cloudnumbers.com is an infrastructure, not a packaged parallelism strategy. It's up to the researcher to choose and set up their tools—perhaps some of the topics we cover in this book—to take advantage of the hardware. We nonetheless feel this is worth mention because it is closely related to this book's topic. You can find out more at *http://cloudnumbers.com/*.

---

‡ The upcoming Revolution R Enterprise 5.0 supports 64-bit Red Hat Enterprise Linux 5 in addition to various Windows flavors. For now, though, the cluster backend must run MS Windows HPC Server. A comment in a blog post stats the team has eyes on Linux cluster support: *http://blog.revolutionanalytics.com/2011/07/fast-logistic-regression-big-data.html*.

About the Authors

Q. Ethan McCallum is a consultant, writer, and technology enthusiast, though perhaps not in that order. His work has appeared online on The O'Reilly Network and Java.net, and also in print publications such as *C/C++ Users Journal*, *Doctor Dobb's Journal*, and *Linux Magazine*. In his professional roles, he helps companies to make smart decisions about data and technology.

Stephen Weston has been working in high performance and parallel computing for over 25 years. He was employed at Scientific Computing Associates in the '90s, working on the Linda programming system invented by David Gelernter. He was also a founder of Revolution Computing, leading the development of parallel computing packages for R, including `nws`, `foreach`, `doSNOW`, and `doMC`. He works at Yale University as an HPC Specialist.

About the Authors

Get even more for your money.

Join the O'Reilly Community, and register the O'Reilly books you own. It's free, and you'll get:

- $4.99 ebook upgrade offer
- 40% upgrade offer on O'Reilly print books
- Membership discounts on books and events
- Free lifetime updates to ebooks and videos
- Multiple ebook formats, DRM FREE
- Participation in the O'Reilly community
- Newsletters
- Account management
- 100% Satisfaction Guarantee

Signing up is easy:

1. **Go to: oreilly.com/go/register**
2. **Create an O'Reilly login.**
3. **Provide your address.**
4. **Register your books.**

Note: English-language books only

To order books online:
oreilly.com/store

For questions about products or an order:
orders@oreilly.com

To sign up to get topic-specific email announcements and/or news about upcoming books, conferences, special offers, and new technologies:
elists@oreilly.com

For technical questions about book content:
booktech@oreilly.com

To submit new book proposals to our editors:
proposals@oreilly.com

O'Reilly books are available in multiple DRM-free ebook formats. For more information:
oreilly.com/ebooks

O'REILLY®

Spreading the knowledge of innovators   oreilly.com

The information you need, when and where you need it.

With Safari Books Online, you can:

Access the contents of thousands of technology and business books

- Quickly search over 7000 books and certification guides
- Download whole books or chapters in PDF format, at no extra cost, to print or read on the go
- Copy and paste code
- Save up to 35% on O'Reilly print books
- **New!** Access mobile-friendly books directly from cell phones and mobile devices

Stay up-to-date on emerging topics before the books are published

- Get on-demand access to evolving manuscripts.
- Interact directly with authors of upcoming books

Explore thousands of hours of video on technology and design topics

- Learn from expert video tutorials
- Watch and replay recorded conference sessions

Spreading the knowledge of innovators   safari.oreilly.com

9 781449 309923